A Childcare and Head Start Center Director's Guide
and Workbook For Leading An Effective Program

I0559541

Stability
at the
Start

ENHANCING TEACHER RETENTION IN EARLY CHILDHOOD EDUCATION

Dr. Bernadine F. Martinez

Copyright © 2024 by Dr. Bernadine Martinez

All rights reserved. No part of this publication may be reproduced, distributed, or transmitted in any form or by any means, including photocopying, recording, or other electronic or mechanical methods, without the prior written permission of the publisher, except in the case of brief quotations embodied in critical reviews and certain other noncommercial uses permitted by copyright law.

Hemingway Publishers 2024

All Rights Reserved

Published by Hemingway Publishers

Cover design by Hemingway Publishers

ISBN: Printed in the United States

Table of Contents

ACKNOWLEDGEMENTS

This dedication is a testament to the love, support, and encouragement I have received from my incredible husband, Arthur Martinez, and my beautiful parents, Rosa and Robert Trevino. Without them, this journey would not have been possible.

To my dearest husband, Arthur, you have been my rock and my pillar of strength. When the weight of the world seemed too much to bear, you were there, holding my hand and reminding me of my own perseverance. Especially midway through this journey, when we found out that I was in stage 4 renal failure. Your relentless belief in me has given me the courage to keep pushing forward, even when I doubted myself the most. Thank you for being my constant source of inspiration and for loving me unconditionally.

To my wonderful parents, Rose and Robert Trevino, you have always been by my side, no matter my rebellious decisions. Your unwavering faith in my abilities has fueled my determination to overcome any obstacle that came my way.

To the rest of my family, friends, and veteran sisters, thank you for your unwavering support and for standing by my side through thick and thin. Your words of encouragement and acts of kindness have uplifted me in ways words cannot express. For my family, I sincerely appreciate your understanding over the past few years of postponing family gatherings and not spending quality time with you. You have shown me the true meaning of family, and I am blessed to have each and every one of you in my life.

PREFACE

"The only thing that is constant is change." - Heraclitus.

In a world where change is the only constant, the field of early childhood education, particularly within Head Start programs, experiences its unique set of transformations. The challenges of high teacher attrition due to factors such as low pay, inadequate support, heavy workload, and poor communication are persistent hurdles. These obstacles not only affect the morale of our educators but also hinder our goal of providing quality education to our young learners. It is within this context of change and challenge that this book was conceived. Its purpose is to empower early childhood directors and professionals with innovative strategies that foster an enriching, supportive workplace culture conducive to retaining top teaching talent despite the prevalent constraints of limited resources.

Given my background as an educator, leader, and advocate for continuous improvement in teaching and learning, the decision to write this book came from witnessing firsthand the struggles faced by early childhood directors and teachers. From conversations with peers to observing the direct impact of high staff turnover on children's learning environments, the stories shared with me underscored the urgent need for a definitive guide that navigates the intricacies of teacher retention in early childhood programs. In addition to my work in other educational leadership roles in school systems, my experiences in various Head Start leadership capacities have deepened my awareness of the complex nature of these issues. This book distills those learnings into actionable insights, aiming to transform a leader's approach to nurturing and retaining their teaching staff.

Through this journey, I have been profoundly inspired by the resilience and dedication of educators who, despite facing significant challenges, remain committed to making a difference in the lives of young learners. I am equally grateful for the support and encouragement I received from colleagues, mentors, and the countless early childhood professionals I've had the privilege to work with. Their stories and experiences have been invaluable in shaping the perspectives and solutions presented in this book.

To the early childhood directors and professionals who find themselves grappling with high teacher turnover, this book is written for you. It seeks to equip you with practical strategies and tools to navigate and overcome the challenges you face. While some familiarity with Head Start programs and early childhood education principles will be beneficial, the book is designed to be accessible to a broad audience, regardless of background.

In these pages, you will find a blueprint—a guide that transcends theoretical discourse, offering instead a pragmatic approach filled with real-world examples, strategies, and worksheets. These resources are intended to aid in understanding the root causes of teacher attrition and also to empower you with the knowledge to build a more supportive, engaging, and sustainable teaching environment.

At the heart of the vibrant educational ecosystem that is early childhood lies a persistent challenge: retaining dedicated teachers. This book is derived from my previous scholarly deliverable, **"Even Though Students Are Getting A Head Start, Why Aren't Teachers Finishing the Race?"** I delve into how nurturing leadership within these programs, coupled with appropriate teacher preparation, sustains these vital educational environments.

I extend my deepest gratitude to you for choosing to invest your time and attention in this work. Your dedication to bettering the lives of both your staff and the children in your care is a testament to the vital role you play in shaping the future. I invite you to continue reading and to join me on this transformational journey. Together, let's uncover the solutions that await us at the culmination of these pages.

HISTORY

A brief history... The Head Start federal program, established in 1965, is one of the nation's most extensive early childhood education programs created to break the cycle of poverty by providing comprehensive educational services to families in need (Office of Head Start, 2021). The program began as "an 8-week demonstration project... that provided preschool children from low-income families with comprehensive... and educational needs" given by volunteers (Office of Head Start - An Office of the Administration for Children and Families, 2021, para. 3). As the program grew, in 1975, Sargent Shriver, former Director of the Office of Economic Opportunity from 1964 to 1968 (Hudson, 2015), and a panel created the Head Start Standards to govern the program. However, the standards did not identify teacher qualifications (as cited in Office of Head Start, 2021). In the past 50 years, administrations have taken steps to improve the program by passing legislative bills to add teacher qualifications, increase funding, and implement systems to ensure the efficient use of resources and enhance service quality (Office of Head Start, 2021).

In an effort to improve educational service standards, the Head Start program has since been expanded and altered by legislation multiple times. In 1998, bipartisan legislation specified that by September 2003, at least 50% of Head Start educators nationally in center-based programs would obtain an "A.A., B.A., or graduate degree in early childhood education... " or related profession to improve the quality of classroom instruction (Hart & Schumacher, 2005, p. 5). According to a 2007 revision and reauthorization of Head Start, at least 50% of Head Start teachers nationwide in center-based programs must possess a bachelor's degree or higher degree in early childhood education by September 30, 2013 (U.S. Department of Health and Human Services, 2007, para. (2)(A)(i)).

According to the Office of Head Start Program Information Report of 2022, 57.75% of the teachers in the nation have attained a B.A. in early childhood education, and 12.38% of the teachers have a B.A. in another field with "coursework equivalent to a major relating to early childhood education with experience teaching preschool-aged children" (U.S. Department of Health & Human Services, 2022, p. 2). Comparably, on the state level in Texas, a prekindergarten teacher must achieve a bachelor's degree in early childhood education or special education, a teaching certification, and an additional qualification to meet the high-quality criteria to teach in a classroom (Education Code Chapter 29. Educational Programs, Sec. 29.167. 2021). According to Hart and Schumacher (2005), teachers with more education in early childhood development may improve results for preschool children.

Teachers voluntarily leaving the profession at high rates in Head Start programs continues to be an issue. According to Wells (2015), poor pay, a lack of training, and high-level responsibilities all contribute to the high turnover rates of Head Start teachers, which restricts the potential beneficial results that may be provided to the children and their families. Although Head Start has gradually increased the teaching qualifications (Office of Head Start - an Office of the Administration for Children and Families, 2021), the rate of pay has not been maintained, and Head Start educators are aware that they will continue to live at the poverty level (Myers, 2021). The Program Information Report from the Office of Head Start Enterprise System (2022) reported that 1,484 Head Start teachers in Texas left the program. Of those teachers, 24.25% left for higher pay in a similar role, 28.32% moved to the state prekindergarten or other early childhood education (ECE) program, and 48.37% changed their career field for unrelated reasons (p.6).

According to Smith et al. (2020), a person's social identities, viewpoints, and cultural practices are intimately linked to their positionality. As a former elementary school principal and early childhood director in an independent school district that was a Head Start grantee, I am aware of the leadership responsibilities for managing a Head Start grant in an exempt program. Additionally, I have worked as an assistant superintendent of education and a regional director for non-profit licensed Head Start programs. Having worked in these two different roles, I found that Head Start center directors lacked sufficient leadership training. In order to better understand how leadership preparation affects attrition among Head Start teachers, I conducted research to learn more about the opinions of both seasoned and inexperienced center directors.

OUR MISSION

The lack of published research on Head Start and early childhood leadership capacity and the absence of support systems, such as an early childhood leadership framework, makes it challenging to provide a solid structure to prepare and educate center directors. This guide is a result of a study aimed at investigating the multiple factors leading to high attrition rates in the early childhood education teaching field in early childhood programs and the relationship this attrition has on the leadership capacity of the program. Studying the underlying factors influencing the high attrition rates could provide policymakers with data to support the need for immediate attention to the early childhood leadership and educator career field.

At my core, I am driven by a deep passion for education and a firm belief in the power of early childhood development. My mission is to empower early childcare leaders and educators through innovative strategies, compassionate guidance, and continuous learning opportunities. We believe that by providing effective leadership training and support, we can create a positive impact on the quality of care and education within childcare centers.

CENTER DIRECTOR HISTORY

Even though various administrations have taken steps over the past 50 years to improve the Head Start program by passing legislative bills to add teacher qualifications, increase funding, and implement systems to ensure the efficient use of resources and enhance service quality. The center director's preparation and significance have been overlooked (Office of Head Start - an Office of the Administration for Children and Families, 2021). Lieberman (2017) identifies most policy change has been focused on teachers, and "much less attention has been paid to leaders" (p. 5). While center directors are essentially completing the same profession as prekindergarten principals, they are not prepared nor supported similarly. Lieberman (2017) concluded that "state licensing standards... tend to have minimal requirements for center director education and training that do not reflect the complexity of the job" (p.30).

Are you a new or novice center director coming from a background different from early childhood? Whether you have experience in childcare, early childhood education, or even another supervisory role, this guide is here to support you on your journey as a center director.

We understand that stepping into this role may feel both exciting and challenging. That's why we've compiled practical strategies to help you lead a high-quality, comprehensive Head Start or childcare program. With legal requirements as a map and philosophical principles as a compass, directors set the course for an entire center. This guide not only outlines these responsibilities but delves into how to manage within the constraints while pushing the boundaries of what's possible.

We'll provide you with valuable insights from other center directors and on best practices. Plus, we'll lead you in creating a nurturing and educational environment that meets the unique needs of your staff, children, and families.

Get ready to embark on an incredible adventure in education! Let's dive in together and make a difference in the lives of young learners.

CHAPTER 1

UNDERSTANDING THE IMPACT OF TEACHER ATTRITION IN EARLY CHILDOOD PROGRAMS

BACKGROUND

The rays of an early morning sun filtered through the classroom windows, casting long, lazy shadows over the vacant centers. Evelyn stood by her desk, thumbing through a stack of construction paper artwork. Each piece was as bright and unique as the child who had created it, unsullied by the complexities of life beyond the Head Start program's walls.

The warmth of the room could not dispel the chill of worry that clung to her. Teacher turnover at the school had reached a point where names and faces in the staff room changed as frequently as the seasons. The impact on the children, a silent cry against the inconsistency, gnawed at her. How could they establish trust when their mentors disappeared without warning?

 A murmur from the corner where the building blocks lay interrupted her ruminations; little Tommy had arrived early again, transported from his challenging home life into the sanctuary of her classroom. His eager eyes often searched for the one permanent figure in his sea of ever-changing caretakers.

His eager eyes often searched for the one permanent figure in his sea of ever-changing caretakers.

Evelyn's heart clenched as she watched him, contemplating the deep-seated effects of the teacher attrition on these vulnerable minds. The invisible threads of attachment they began to weave with each new teacher were often torn out before they could be tightened, leaving frayed ends of what could have been a tapestry of trust and learned security.

She remembered Ms. Harrow, Tommy's favorite teacher, who had left mid-semester for a better-paying job. Evelyn thought back to Tommy's confusion and heard his simple question again: "Where did Ms. Harrow go? Will she come back to play with me?" She didn't have the words then, and she didn't have them now.

Conversations with other teachers had yielded a plethora of well-meaning advice and hushed frustrations. These dialogues were incipient steps toward knitting a community of educators determined to staunch the flow of peers walking out the door. Evelyn mulled over the balance between the visceral satisfaction of teaching these young minds and the cold reality of financial survival that compelled their instructors away.

A soft shuffle of tiny feet drew her attention back to Tommy, who now looked up at her expectantly, the burgeoning light of the morning not quite reaching the corners of his anxious eyes. Could a stable, supportive environment be cultured in this climate of constant change, she wondered, as she knelt beside him and began to build towers from the colorful wooden blocks.

The thought that perhaps today's efforts might yield the blueprint for a more hopeful tomorrow flickered in her mind. What actions could she take to ensure that this blueprint became a reality, to foster a nurturing learning ecosystem where both teacher and child could flourish?

A CRISIS IN THE CLASSROOM: THE SILENT TOLL OF TEACHER TURNOVER

In these next few chapters, we begin with understanding attrition factors such as compensation, job satisfaction, workplace challenges, social support, and professional development. We'll dive into the factors that contribute to high turnover rates and identify strategies for addressing them. Our goal is to equip you, the center director or administrator, with the tools and resources needed to thrive in your career and create a positive impact in your center or school. So let's get started! Remember, we're in this together. Let's learn and grow towards greatness.

High teacher attrition in childcare programs is more than a human resources issue—it's a growing crisis that directly undermines the educational and emotional foundation of our youngest learners. Stability and consistency are not mere educational buzzwords; they are indispensable conditions for effective teaching and meaningful learning in early childhood. Within these pages, we confront the complexities of teacher turnover and its trickle-down effect on the developmental journeys of children in childcare programs. The journey to transform this trend starts with a deep understanding of the problem at hand.

In the face of disheartening statistics showing alarmingly high rates of teacher attrition across childcare settings, it becomes clear that retaining dedicated educators is not merely an operational challenge but a moral imperative. When a teacher leaves, it's not just a classroom that's affected—it's a child's worldview that might be shaken. Continuity is as crucial to a child's early education as the curriculum itself, and the loss of a teacher can have far-reaching impacts on this delicate ecosystem. In the first chapter, we will explore how teacher attrition leads to a breakdown in the stability and consistency of education delivery. This critical component can disrupt learning and create a cascade of challenges.

With the absence of familiar faces and the introduction of new teaching styles, children can experience confusion and stress that may go unnoticed or underestimated by adults. We delve into how these frequent disruptions can impair **social-emotional development**, one of the central pillars of Head Start's mission. By identifying the repercussions of teacher turnover, we can begin to understand the developmental consequences for the most affected party—the children.

Yet beyond understanding the problem lies the heart of this book: the mission to cultivate a more **stable and supportive environment**. This is where we recognize the importance of improving teacher retention and providing leadership support, not as an end in itself but as a means to elevate educational quality and provide children with the nurturing environment they deserve. Real transformation requires that we not only keep our teachers but also empower them to become leaders who can flourish within—and contribute to—their communities.

This chapter sets the stage for a compelling narrative that unfolds throughout the book, connecting the glaring issue of high teacher turnover with actionable strategies early childhood leaders and education professionals. The core challenge of teacher attrition is multifaceted, with roots in low pay, overbearing workloads, inadequate support systems, and lack of communication, which we will meticulously dissect. Empowering our readers with knowledge and strategies, we provide a practical framework to tackle these systemic issues head-on without falling prey to the often-cited constraint of limited resources and support.

Readers will emerge with a holistic perspective on how teacher turnover threatens the fabric of childcare programs and the actionable insights to transform this unsettling pattern. This chapter will not only lay out the distressing implications of high attrition rates but also shine a light on the path forward: a methodical approach toward positive change that can commence within a few months to a year.

With a combination of research, case studies, and forward-thinking methodologies, we will chart a course for sustainable improvement in teacher retention. Take the next steps toward evolving from understanding to action, from instability to continuity, and from leadership challenges to confident educational stewardship. Together, we will forge a new paradigm in which our youngest generation can thrive, supported by educators who are as committed to their careers as they are to their student's futures.

High teacher attrition in childcare programs has a profoundly negative impact on the stability and consistency of education delivery. When teachers leave at high rates, it results in a constant cycle of instability within the program. This instability not only affects the educators themselves but also disrupts the learning environment for the children. For instance, when there is a high turnover of teachers, it becomes challenging to maintain a consistent curriculum, teaching style, and disciplinary approach. This inconsistency can lead to confusion and anxiety among the children, hindering their ability to learn and thrive in the classroom.

Furthermore, high teacher attrition compromises the establishment of a supportive and nurturing relationship between educators and children. **When teachers are constantly leaving, it disrupts the development of trust and rapport, which is essential for an optimal learning environment.** Students may struggle to form attachments to their teachers and may also experience added stress when having to adapt to new personalities and teaching styles regularly. This constant upheaval in the classroom creates an emotionally tumultuous environment, hindering the children's emotional and intellectual growth.

Additionally, high teacher turnover disrupts the development of a cohesive team within the program. The departure of experienced staff members erodes the knowledge base and interconnectedness that is key to creating a successful and efficient learning environment. **It can take time for new staff members to acclimate to the program and bond with their colleagues, which further delays the stability needed to provide consistent and high-quality education.** As a result, the integrity of the program's collaborative framework is jeopardized, impacting both teachers and students alike.

Moreover, the financial cost of high teacher attrition cannot be overlooked. The constant need to recruit, hire, and onboard new teachers consumes precious time and resources. It also disrupts the flow of the program's operations, leading to potential gaps in coverage and support for the children. This ultimately affects the overall quality of education and the ability of the program to serve its purpose effectively.

Recognizing and understanding the detrimental impact of high teacher attrition is the first step toward creating a more stable and consistent learning environment for the children in childcare programs. Let's delve deeper into the developmental impacts of teacher attrition on the children and recognize the urgent need for retaining top teaching talent in our next section.

High teacher attrition in childcare programs can have profound developmental impacts on the children under their care. When teachers leave at a high rate, it disrupts the establishment of meaningful and consistent relationships between teachers and students, which are crucial in early childhood education. Consistency is vital for a child's sense of security and trust, and **when teachers depart frequently, it can lead to feelings of distress and insecurity among the children.**

Young children thrive on routines and stability, and consistent relationships with their caregivers play a significant role in their emotional and social development. With high teacher turnover, the children in these programs often experience a loss of connection, making it challenging for them to form trusting relationships with their new teachers.

Moreover, the **impact of teacher attrition on children's cognitive development is substantial**. As children are in the critical stage of early brain development, being exposed to consistent learning experiences is essential. Frequent turnover disrupts the consistency in teaching methods and learning environments, which can lead to developmental setbacks for the children.

The lack of stability resulting from high teacher attrition can even lead to increased behavioral issues in children. The uncertainty and transitions caused by frequent turnover create an environment where children may struggle to regulate their emotions and behavior. **Children may exhibit signs of anxiety, clinginess, or acting out due to the disruption in their daily interactions and routines.**

Furthermore, the turnover of teachers can also impact the educational progress of the children. As new teachers acclimate to the classroom and the curriculum, there is often a period of adjustment that can affect the continuity of learning. This transient period can result in some children falling behind or missing out on vital educational opportunities.

In essence, the developmental impacts of teacher attrition in early childhood programs are multi-faceted and pervasive, affecting the emotional, social, cognitive, and behavioral development of the children. Recognizing these detrimental effects is crucial in understanding the urgency of addressing teacher retention in order to provide a stable and nurturing environment for the children in these programs.

Teacher retention is pivotal to fostering a stable and supportive learning landscape. The value of retaining experienced and passionate educators cannot be overstated. **Consistency** is the foundation upon which young learners build trust and a sense of safety, enabling them to explore, engage, and ultimately succeed in their educational pursuits. When teachers remain in their positions long-term, they cultivate deeper relationships with their students, better understand their individual needs, and tailor the learning experience to foster each child's growth.

Retention of teachers also creates a ripple effect within the educational ecosystem. **Educators who stay** in the program bring a **wealth of knowledge** and experience that benefits new teachers, creating a culture of mentorship and ongoing professional development. This internal support network is crucial, given the complexities and unique challenges faced in early childhood environments. It enables educators to share best practices, strategies for engagement, and behavior management techniques that are particularly effective in supporting at-risk children.

Administrative stability is another advantage that comes with high teacher retention rates. Directors and other leaders are able to focus on strategic initiatives and program enhancements when they are not overwhelmed by the need to recruit and train new staff constantly. As a result, the entire program operates more effectively and efficiently – with seasoned teachers contributing to the decision-making process and helping to implement improvements that directly contribute to student outcomes.

From an operational standpoint, reducing teacher turnover is **cost-effective.** The financial burden of advertising, hiring, and training new teachers is significant, and the resources required to onboard new staff can instead be allocated toward enriching the program and investing in resources that directly affect student learning. Moreover, the continuity of staff allows for a more predictable and well-managed budget, empowering directors to plan further ahead and make more strategic investments in their programs.

Teacher retention also contributes to a **positive organizational culture**, one that values collaboration, continuity, and commitment. This environment nurtures professional growth, where teachers feel supported and valued, leading to improved job satisfaction and morale.

When teachers are happy and engaged in their work, it translates to a more vibrant and dynamic classroom setting, which directly benefits students.

Improving teacher retention is a complex issue, but it is essential for the well-being of both educators and students. To tackle this challenge, directors and early childhood professionals must understand the factors contributing to teacher turnover and actively pursue strategies that address them. Offering competitive salaries, professional development opportunities, a supportive community, and recognition of teachers' contributions are all strategies that have been shown to improve retention.

In sum, the central role of teacher retention cannot be overstated. It is the linchpin that holds together the quality and consistency of education delivery, the development of a collaborative and supportive culture, and the overall success of the program. As we delve into the various dimensions of this critical issue, let us remember that at the heart of this effort are the children who stand to gain the most from the stability and dedication of their teachers.

In this chapter, we explored the tip of the iceberg of the detrimental effects of high teacher attrition on the stability and consistency of education delivery. We also explored the developmental impacts of teacher attrition on the children in these programs. Finally, we emphasized the importance of improving teacher retention to create a stable and supportive environment for both teachers and students.

Understanding the negative impact of high teacher attrition is essential for early childhood directors and educators. It directly affects the stability and quality of education, leading to inconsistencies that can impede the children's learning and development.

The **developmental impacts of teacher attrition on the children** are significant. Constant turnover of teachers can disrupt the trust, relationships, and routine that are crucial for a child's sense of security and learning.

Recognizing the **importance of improving teacher retention** is paramount for creating a stable and supportive environment for both teachers and students. It not only ensures a consistent and nurturing learning environment for children but also contributes to the professional growth and job satisfaction of the teachers.

As we move forward in this book, readers can expect a comprehensive exploration of strategies and solutions aimed at transforming the landscape of teacher retention and leadership support. By addressing these challenges, early childhood directors and educators can cultivate an environment where both teachers and students thrive. Through actionable insights and real-world examples, this book offers a blueprint for creating a positive and impactful change.

The journey ahead holds the promise of empowering early childhood professionals to build a thriving, supportive environment and retain top teaching talent without the common struggle of limited resources and support.

CHAPTER 2

RESEARCH BEHIND
ATTRITION FACTORS

BACKGROUND

Every child's potential blooms best in an environment of support and challenge. What does it take to create such a space? In this chapter, we shift our gaze towards building a strong foundation for teacher retention through enhancing teacher stability. We examine the research on job satisfaction, social support, professional development, and more.

As educators, we often face challenges that may lead to feelings of burnout and, ultimately, attrition. These can include high workloads, lack of support from administration, challenging students or classroom environments, and a lack of professional development opportunities. It's important to recognize these factors and address them within our centers in order to create a positive and sustainable work environment.

 So why is it important to address these challenges? For one, as explained in chapter 1, high turnover rates can have a significant impact on the quality of education and the overall success of a center or school. When teachers leave, there's a disruption in continuity for students, creating a loss of trust and stability. Additionally, hiring and training new staff can be time-consuming and costly. By addressing the root causes of attrition, we can create a more stable and supportive environment for teachers, leading to improved student outcomes and overall success for our centers.

Throughout this section, we'll provide research, resources, and strategies for addressing teacher attrition factors. We encourage you to reflect on your own center or school's practices and see where improvements can be made. Let's work together to create a positive work culture.

WHAT DRIVES TEACHER ATTRITION?

The issues that cause educators to leave their positions are multifaceted. While salary disparities between early childhood teachers and K-12 teachers are frequently cited as a primary driver, it is far from the only one. More deeply ingrained concerns such as inadequate professional development opportunities, high-stress levels, lack of autonomy in lesson planning, and lack of support from administration are also prominent factors. Furthermore, the often under-resourced and challenging environments in which early childhood teachers work can compound these problems. Addressing these issues requires a multi-faceted approach that tackles both the external factors and internal challenges.

UNDERSTANDING THE IMPORTANCE OF TEACHER RETENTION

The high turnover rate among early childhood teachers has far-reaching consequences beyond just filling vacancies and having a warm body-for ratio (a recipe for disaster). High teacher turnover can have a negative impact on children's learning outcomes, safety in and out of the classroom, as well as school culture and community relationships. It can also result in increased costs for recruiting, hiring, and training new teachers. Moreover, the loss of experienced teachers means losing valuable knowledge and expertise that could have been beneficial to the program. Prioritizing teacher retention not only benefits the teachers themselves but it also has a positive ripple effect on the entire community.

Attrition is an enemy of stability and growth. What causes good teachers to leave, and how can directors foster the conditions to make them stay? The next few pages explain the factors of attrition.

Unfortunately, the lack of teacher qualifications is the tip of the iceberg. In a study, Jeon and Wells (2018) examined the Early Childhood Job Attitude Survey psychometrics and its capacity to offer valuable data for early childhood education research and practice. The study's second objective was to determine if organizational-level variables could be utilized to forecast teacher turnover. Jeon and Wells stated that "knowing which organizational-level factors impact turnover can aid researchers and practitioners toward utilizing preventative strategies to decrease turnover" (p. 565). The study explored whether different aspects of teachers' attitudes were associated with teacher turnover. They studied the attitudes of early childhood education (ECE) teachers from an organizational perspective. The three characteristics of "workplace satisfaction, classroom responsibilities, and ongoing support" were explored (p. 567). Workplace contentment was the only one of the three criteria that accurately predicted early childhood teachers' actual turnover. The workplace satisfaction component captured a degree of the teacher's feelings and thoughts about the program and job. Jean and Wells (2018) discovered that a positive working connection with the director was a sign of contented teachers. Jeon and Wells concluded that one way to decrease teacher turnover is to understand the reasons for teacher turnover and to increase teachers' job attitudes and satisfaction.

In another study, Brill and McCartney (2008) addressed heavy workloads, poor leadership, and inadequate administrative support, attributing to the cause of high attrition rates in early childhood programs, and they reviewed methods of increasing teacher retention. Their research indicated teacher attrition was due to low salaries, lack of social input, and student discipline problems. Additionally, they claimed that high attrition rates had a detrimental impact on working relationships and had institutional costs, such as the funds lost for training teachers. These high institutional costs increase the fiscal budget. According to Brill and McCartney (2008):

As trained teachers leave their schools, a double loss occurs: money has been lost in training that will not be applied as a tool for improvement at that particular school, and more money has to be spent on the training of incoming teachers. (p. 753)

In terms of instruction, when teachers leave, there are negative implications for student achievement; schools in high-minority populations are hit twice.

Brill and McCartney (2008) further explained the causes of teachers leaving the profession involved class size, workload, student behaviors, leadership and administration, facilities and resources, maternity, poor mentoring, and low salary. Their solutions to the issue were increasing teacher salaries, recruiting talented teachers, improving work environments, implementing or improving professional communities, and creating or improving mentoring programs. Brill and McCartney also discovered that the interaction between new and experienced teachers was the most important aspect of induction programs. In a variety of areas, such as "pedagogy, classroom management, lesson planning, and emotional support," mentors provide new teachers with critical assistance and guidance (p. 767).

JOB SATISFACTION

Collie et al. (2012) found that "if teachers have confidence in their ability to engage students, manage the classroom, and use effective instructional strategies, the impact of student behavior stress did not appear to relate negatively to job satisfaction" (p. 1199). So, what does this mean? Collie et al. encouraged school administration to provide quality in-service training to teachers that addresses the tools necessary to effectively manage their classrooms. As a result, positive job satisfaction will lead to lower turnover rates.

In another study, Carson et al. (2016) conducted a study to examine "how the feelings of exhaustion throughout the day relate to the perception of end-of-day job satisfaction and quitting intentions" (p. 801). For one week during the autumn semester of school, the researchers gave 50 instructors the **Ecological Momentary Assessment**, a self-assessment that gauged the teacher's daily observations of sensations of weariness three times a day. In addition to the assessment, the teachers were provided with a list of rejuvenating strategies they could implement during the day to relieve stress and if it impacted their thoughts or feelings on "job satisfaction and quitting intentions" (p. 803). As a result, Carson et al. had three significant findings. First, it was revealed that the more exhaustion teachers had by the end of the day, the less job satisfaction and more intentions of quitting their jobs were true. Second, it was found that they had less job stress if teachers took advantage of the rejuvenating exercise. Finally, they found that physical and cognitive reprieve strategies were more effective than proactive professionalism or adult communication. Carson et al. encouraged leaders to integrate activities into place and schedule time for teachers' participation.

Edinger and Edinger (2018) surveyed elementary teachers in two rural southeastern school districts in the United States. The surveys measured teacher efficacy, perceived organizational support, coworker relationships, and job satisfaction. As a result, the researchers found that "higher levels of trust… higher levels of teacher efficacy were related to significantly higher levels of job satisfaction" (p. 584). They also found that teacher effectiveness and job satisfaction are strongly related to greater perceived organizational support. The research has substantial implications for leadership because they play a vital role in "helping teachers develop trust and job satisfaction" (p. 587).

In an international study, Skaalvik and Skaalvik (2011) examined the "relations between school context variables and teachers' feeling of belonging, emotional exhaustion, job satisfaction, and motivation to leave the teaching profession" by evaluating 2569 elementary and middle school, Norwegian teachers (p. 1030). Using the AMOS 7 program, they measured value consonance, supervisor support, relationships with coworkers, relationships with parents, time pressure, and discipline issues. Skaalvik and Skaalvik found that "both teachers' feelings of belonging and emotional exhaustion were predictive of job satisfaction while emotional exhaustion and job satisfaction were predictive of motivation to leave the teaching profession" (p. 1036). This study concluded that school administrators must focus more on teachers' job happiness, emotional exhaustion, and sense of belonging.

CHALLENGES TO JOB SATISFACTION

Further research led to an understanding of how federal mandates could increase the stress factors associated with job satisfaction. Jacoby and Lesaux (2017) organized a longitudinal study of Head Start teachers and how they responded to the educational mandates established by Head Start. Twenty Head Start teachers were interviewed by the researchers. The researchers found that 18 of the 20 teachers had difficulty implementing the mandated curriculum with fidelity due to daily interruptions such as the social-emotional and immediate needs of the children. They added that they felt constrained and could not meet the needs of the students in their classrooms because they were required to submit their lesson plans to their education mentors to ensure that they adhered to strict instructional mandates. This imbalance between administrative duties and classroom duties caused stress for the teachers.

In addition to federal mandates, the additional workloads and tasks not associated with the job description could lead to negative job satisfaction. Eatough et al. (2015) examined illegitimate tasks and their effects on a person's well-being. They reported "the results of two daily diary studies, one in which 57 Swiss employees were assessed twice/daily and one in which 90 Americans were assessed three times/day" (p. 108). They explained that illegitimate tasks are additional tasks outside their job descriptions assigned to employees that make them feel below their pay level. These tasks include duties such as but are not limited to, sweeping, mopping, cleaning toilets, cooking, and cleaning trash cans. As a result of the findings, Eatough et al. concluded that "illegitimate tasks were most consistently related to anger and job satisfaction" (p. 122).

Similarly, in research by Apostel et al. (2018) examining illegitimate tasks, they found that continuously assigning illegitimate tasks direct correlated with turnover intention. Both research studies imply that management should be cautious about how many additional tasks are assigned to individuals outside their designated duties, which could cause stress, anger, and job dissatisfaction, leading to turnover.

In a separate study, Eatough et al. (2015) measured the effects of illegitimate tasks on self-esteem. These findings imply that leaders should be mindful of the possibility that some duties may be viewed as being unjustified. Managers should undoubtedly concentrate on completing the required tasks; however, they should think about the message that their assignments convey. Open instances of humiliation or indignity are frequently simple to identify and, if acknowledged, are more easily avoided or corrected.

SOCIAL SUPPORT

Thus far, attributes leading to job satisfaction have helped us understand why teachers leave the profession. Nevertheless, another factor, teacher support, was highly mentioned in many studies (Delali et al., 2020; McMullen et al., 2020; Pomaki et al., 2010). One study by Pomaki et al. (2010) examined the role of social support in turnover intention among new teachers. Seventy-one new teachers in Canada were asked to participate in a study at the beginning of the school year. The researchers discovered that teachers who received social support from mentor teachers, center directors, or other seasoned educators were less likely to quit their employment. It was also found that higher workloads would not be a significant factor for teacher turnover if it was combined with social support. It was also stated that "social support must offer the person what is needed to deal with the stressor successfully and has to come from a source that can be helpful with that particular stressor" (p. 1344). The research concluded that programs should investigate implementing systems that foster and support teachers.

In another study, McMullen et al. (2020) examined teachers' general well-being and the implications of turnover by measuring three categories; "supportive structures, collegial relationships, and professional beliefs and values" (p. 340). The three categories were calculated by the nine senses of early childhood professional well-being in the Early Childhood Professional Well-being Model, based on Maslow's Hierarchy of Needs. In the study, the researchers obtained a convenience sample of 218 early childhood professionals from three early childhood organizations by sending an anonymous online link via email and published in a magazine. As a result, they found that the area of supportive structures (sense of engagement, sense of agency, sense of comfort, sense of security, sense of efficacy, sense of communication, sense of contribution) in the three questionnaires submitted resulted in less job satisfaction, and the risk of turnover was predictive. Collegial relationships were not a predictor of leaving the profession. Lastly, the third category of professional beliefs and values resulted in a feeling of autonomy, making choices, or feeling respected, which leads to more job satisfaction. McMullen et al. (2020) suggested that "the well-being of early childhood professionals is indeed a matter of quality insofar as it is associated with the risk of turnover" (p. 342).

Similarly, Delali et al. (2020) investigated the relationship between teacher emotions, emotional labor, and teacher burnout, resulting in the intention to quit in an international study. The study was carried out with a total of 628 surveyed Ghanaian teachers. They discovered variables such as deep acting, surface feelings, hiding feelings, and social support. The results indicated a mixture of results. Delali et al. found that solid team support leads to teachers being able to cope with work stressors and the depletion of resources.

However, concerning emotional labor, they stated, "respondents mostly applied the hiding emotions in the performance of their duties, followed by deep acting and faking," which is a direct correlation to burnout leading to an intention to quit (p. 136). The results indicate that leaders should focus on creating a support team, implementing coaching programs, and providing professional development to build capacity and self-regulation strategies.

TEACHER PREPARATION AND PROFESSIONAL DEVELOPMENT

Teachers' capacity for growth is constrained when they are not exposed to teaching, training, and professional growth. This lack of knowledge affects their self-esteem and self-actualization. Self-actualization is the final level of Maslow's theory of human motivation. Maslow (1943) defined self-actualization as the ideal state in which one makes the best use of their gifts. The lack of professional development is a significant source of frustration for teachers. For this reason, it is crucial for center directors to provide staff with professional development throughout the year.

THE IMPORTANCE OF PROFESSIONAL DEVELOPMENT

Professional development is an essential aspect of education, particularly for teachers. It not only helps teachers enhance their teaching skills but also provides them with the latest knowledge and techniques to stay relevant in a constantly evolving educational landscape.

Through professional development, teachers can improve their self-esteem and self-actualization by gaining confidence in their abilities and staying motivated to make a positive impact on their students. It also promotes continuous learning and growth, allowing teachers to develop new strategies and approaches to teaching.

Early childhood leaders and center directors play an important role in providing professional development opportunities for their staff. By doing so, they can empower their educators to provide high-quality early childhood education that meets the changing standards and curriculum requirements.

In conclusion, professional development is crucial for the success of early childhood education. As the landscape of education continues to change, it is vital that educators stay up-to-date and equipped with the best practices and knowledge to support and lay the foundation for early childhood education. Early childhood leaders must prioritize professional development to ensure a bright future for the next generation. So let's continue to invest in our staff.

COMPENSATION AND PAY

The literature identified factors such as qualifications, job satisfaction, social support, and other attributes throughout my study. Low pay and no benefits also lead to teachers leaving the profession, which, according to studies, will affect both the workplace environment and student success (Bullough et al., 2012; Cassidy et al., 2011; Hart & Schumacher, 2005). As defined in the conceptual framework, the theory of human motivation (Maslow, 1943) explains the first basic physiological need as being equitably compensated for one's work and receiving basic medical coverage. Without this, people cannot provide food and shelter on their behalf and offer financial or medical support. Thus leading center directors and educators to find an alternate solution.

A study by Whitebook et al. (2014) contrasted childcare providers with preschool teachers, non-farm animal caregivers, fast food cooks, and bank tellers between 1997 and 2013; they found that "childcare workers earned less than animal caretakers in both years" (p. 16). In comparison, preschool teachers were paid 60% less in hourly wages than kindergarten teachers in 2013. Even when childcare payments more than doubled (Whitebook et al., 2014).

In another study, Cassidy et al. (2011) used the triangulation method of teachers, directors, and parents' experiences of teacher turnover. A mixed-method study using data from classroom observations, interviews, teacher and director self-reports, and researcher field notes was used to better understand the dynamics "of teacher turnover and its implications" for the program (p. 2). They found that low compensation directly resulted in teachers and directors being more likely to leave the occupation. It was also found that turnover increased the workload of teachers and directors. Directors were forced to cover classrooms, which took time away from their administrative duties. The results of teacher turnover also indicated a connection to children's negative behaviors. The interviews and the responses to the survey powerfully revealed that teachers would stay in their present jobs if salaries were increased, benefits provided, and teacher assistance were available. It was also revealed that a negative work environment and lack of support were factors in turnover. Overall, the study revealed how proactive centers could minimize the impact of turnover if they had prepared policies and procedures, a direct reflection of leadership implementing organizational procedures.

Researchers Bridges et al. (2011) conducted a 3-year longitudinal study sampling 2,783 teachers, teacher assistants, teacher aides, and child care directors of private child care, public funding preschool, and Head Start preschools participating in California's Child Care Retention Incentive program. Due to high attrition rates in California, the incentive program was designed to provide monetary incentives and professional development to those who sought college-level courses, thus reducing job turnover. According to the study, participants in the early childhood program were less likely to leave the field after the 3-year program; however, some did get promotions or go into another ECE program that paid more. In contrast, the researchers discovered that in the first 2 years of work, the percentage of Head Start teachers quitting their jobs was substantially greater than in the private centers. This could be due to finding a higher-paying job in the ECE private or public sector. Additionally, "strongest effects on college unit completion were experienced by lower paid staff and Latina aides or teachers" (p. 1025). Finally, participants who started the program with tenure, higher degrees, and higher paying salaries (the first basic physiological need of the theory of human motivation (Maslow, 1943) were less likely to leave the profession than those with lower pay and tenure.

CHAPTER 3

Identifying Root Causes
Of Teacher Attrition

Background

The early morning sun peeked through the classroom windows, casting a warm glow across the room filled with colorful posters, alphabet-lined walls, and tiny chairs. Margaret, a seasoned Head Start director, stood silently amid the quiet before the arrival of chattering children, her mind consumed with a puzzle of attrition that had plagued her program for the past year.

The scent of freshly waxed floors mixed with a hint of crayon wax transported her back to her first years of teaching, a time when enthusiasm bubbled despite scarce resources. But as the years passed, the turnover of dedicated teachers spiraled, leaving her contemplative amidst the stillness. Her heart ached with each resignation letter, troubling her with thoughts of continuity for the children and wavering program quality.

Margaret walked to her desk, her hand grazing over a pile of exit interviews, the paper edges soft from her many reviews searching for answers. The reasons for leaving were as varied as the teachers themselves: burnout, inadequate compensation, and limited professional development opportunities. "How could we nurture these young minds," she thought, "if we couldn't even sustain their teachers?"
The playground's laughter momentarily disrupted her musings. Outside, the teachers—her teachers—wove through games of tag and towers of blocks, their smiles belying the uncertainty of their tenure. Through the pane, she noticed Miss Jenkins, once vibrant, now with a furrow of stress lining her brow. Margaret knew the signs well. The cycle had to be broken.

Resolved, she turned to her computer, pulling up research on teacher retention. She sifted through studies and journals, locating pieces of a complex puzzle: the call for competitive salaries, the importance of supportive work culture, and professional growth paths tailored to individual needs. Innovative solutions took shape in her mind—mentorship programs, stronger community partnerships for teacher support, and policy advocacy for increased funding.

As she scribbled ideas on a yellow pad, her usually stoic face softened into optimism. Each intervention held promise, a step towards a brighter future for her teachers and, consequently, for the children who depended on them.

As the day waned and the murmur of contented fatigue settled among her staff, Margaret pondered, "Could these interventions be enough to stem the tide of teacher departure?" She understood the journey ahead would demand resilience and collaboration, but the well-being of her teachers and the success of the children ignited a passion that was both invigorating and necessary. Would the fabric of their collective efforts hold strong against the strain of attrition, or would the need for more systemic change push them to reinvent the very foundation of their mission?

THE HIDDEN CRISIS IN EARLY CHILDHOOD EDUCATION

Teacher attrition in early childhood programs is a **silent exodus** that drains talent and disrupts the growth and development of young children. Hiring and training a new teacher is not just a line item in a budget; it represents a significant loss of institutional knowledge and affects the cultural and educational fabric of an organization. Understanding these dynamics, particularly in the context of early childhood and Head Start programs, is **crucial for building a resilient teaching workforce.**

By dissecting the causes of this trend, leaders can turn insights into action. A thorough assessment of the attrition factors forms the first step to crafting sustainable interventions. It's not about quick fixes but **identifying systematic issues**—from compensation and working conditions to opportunities for professional development and support systems. Importantly, we must explore how these factors interact with the personal and professional lives of educators.

Empowering teachers is the heart of this transformation. Becoming adept at recognizing **early warning signs** of dissatisfaction or burnout can mean the difference between keeping and losing valuable educators. It requires a proactive approach, one that also considers the intricacies of adult learning styles and the unique demands of teaching early childhood education. The stakes are high; teacher turnover can have a ripple effect, potentially diminishing the quality of education and care provided to our most vulnerable populations.

Strategic leaders understand that **data is their ally**. By harnessing feedback and analytics, an organization can formulate a tangible plan, targeting the underlying causes rather than just the symptoms of attrition. This includes delving into **job satisfaction surveys, exit interviews, and performance metrics**. Such measures help to zoom in on the critical aspects that matter most to educators in their work environment.

Yet, embracing a collaborative culture is perhaps the most critical element. **Inclusivity and equity** go hand in hand with retention. When educators feel valued and heard, they are more likely to remain engaged and committed to their roles. This involves creating avenues for peer support and mentorship alongside fostering diverse perspectives within the leadership and curriculum design. It's not just a strategy but a shift towards a more connected and supportive educational community.

As we journey through this chapter, we aim to equip directors with the tools to conduct an insightful assessment, leading to interventions that resonate on a profound level with educators. You will learn that addressing the root causes of teacher attrition is more than an administrative task—it's a **pathway to rejuvenating passion**, nurturing talent, and, ultimately, **enriching the lives of the children** we serve. With the collective efforts of all stakeholders, these strategies forge a vibrant and stable learning atmosphere where every child benefits from the consistency and expertise of their teachers.

Identifying the factors contributing to teacher attrition is a crucial first step in addressing the challenges faced by early childhood programs. A thorough assessment of these contributing factors enables directors to gain valuable insight into the specific areas that require attention and intervention. By understanding the root causes of attrition, directors can develop targeted strategies to retain top teaching talent and create a supportive environment for both teachers and students.

One key aspect of conducting a thorough assessment is to **analyze** the reasons why teachers leave the program. This could involve **exit interviews, surveys, and data analysis to identify common themes** and patterns. It is essential to go beyond surface-level explanations and delve into the underlying issues that lead to attrition.

Understanding the impact of working conditions, professional development opportunities, leadership support, and work-life balance on teacher retention is also vital. By examining these areas in detail, directors can identify potential areas of improvement and develop tailored interventions to address these challenges effectively.

Furthermore, it's important to take into account the **perspectives** of both current and former teachers. Don't forget the insights from other center directors, whether novice or experienced. Their insights can provide valuable perspectives on the working environment, management practices, and the overall culture of the program. This valuable feedback can guide the development of strategies to enhance teacher retention and wellbeing.

Another crucial aspect of the assessment process is to **analyze** the data related to teacher turnover and retention rates. This data-driven approach can provide directors with concrete evidence of the factors contributing to attrition, making it easier to prioritize areas for improvement and allocate resources effectively.

Additionally, certain external **factors**, such as community dynamics, economic conditions, and demographic shifts, can also impact teacher attrition. Acknowledging and understanding these external influences is essential for developing comprehensive retention strategies that are sensitive to the unique context of early childhood programs.

By conducting a thorough assessment of the contributing factors to teacher attrition, directors can gain a comprehensive understanding of the challenges faced by their program. This knowledge lays the foundation for targeted interventions and strategic initiatives to improve teacher retention and create a supportive and thriving environment for both teachers and students.

IDENTIFY SPECIFIC AREAS THAT REQUIRE ATTENTION TO ADDRESS THE CHALLENGES OF TEACHER ATTRITION.

In order to effectively address the challenges of teacher attrition in early childhood programs, it is crucial to identify the specific areas that require attention. By pinpointing the root causes and contributing factors, early childhood directors can develop targeted interventions that are tailored to the unique needs of their program. This targeted approach allows for a more precise and efficient use of resources, resulting in a greater impact on teacher retention.

As we learned through research, one area that requires attention is **professional development**. Teachers who feel supported in their professional growth are more likely to remain in their positions. Providing opportunities for ongoing training, mentorship, and career advancement can significantly contribute to teacher satisfaction and retention. It's essential for directors to assess current professional development programs and identify areas for improvement or expansion.

Another critical area is **job satisfaction** and **workplace culture**. A positive and supportive workplace culture has a significant impact on teacher retention. Creating an environment where teachers feel valued, heard, and respected can make a substantial difference in their decision to stay or leave. Directors should examine the existing culture within their programs and work towards fostering a collaborative, inclusive, and supportive environment.

Mental and emotional support for teachers is also a crucial area that requires attention. The demands of working in early childhood education can take a toll on teachers' mental and emotional well-being. Offering resources for stress management, counseling services, and emotional support can help teachers cope with the challenges they face and reduce burnout. Directors should consider implementing strategies to support the mental and emotional health of their teaching staff.

Compensation and benefits are fundamental factors in teacher retention. Competitive salary packages, comprehensive benefits, and incentives for continued education can significantly impact a teacher's decision to stay or leave. Conducting a thorough assessment of the current compensation and benefits structure is essential for identifying areas for improvement and making adjustments that align with teachers' needs.

Beyond these areas, it's critical to consider **teacher workload**. Excessive workloads without appropriate support and resources can lead to burnout and dissatisfaction. Directors should evaluate teacher workload and consider ways to streamline responsibilities, offer adequate resources, and create a more sustainable work environment.

Additionally, **communication and feedback** play a crucial role in teacher retention. Open, transparent communication channels and constructive feedback are essential for building trust and fostering a sense of belonging. Directors should assess the effectiveness of communication channels and feedback mechanisms within their programs to ensure that teachers feel heard and valued.

Finally, **leadership support and involvement** are vital for addressing teacher attrition. Strong, supportive leadership can make a significant difference in the job satisfaction and retention of teaching staff. Directors should evaluate their own leadership approach and identify opportunities for providing greater support and involvement in the professional development and well-being of their teachers.

By identifying these specific areas that require attention, early childhood directors can develop targeted interventions to effectively address the root causes of teacher attrition in their programs. This approach enables a more strategic and impactful response to the complex challenges of retaining top teaching talent.

DEVELOPING TARGETED INTERVENTIONS

Developing targeted interventions to effectively address the root causes of teacher attrition requires a nuanced understanding of the unique challenges and stressors that educators in early childhood programs face. With a deep-dive analysis in place, directors can move beyond superficial solutions and implement strategies that truly resonate with the needs of their teachers, leading toward a more stable and committed teaching workforce.

ALIGN INTERVENTIONS WITH IDENTIFIED CHALLENGES

The first step in creating these interventions is to **align them closely with the specific challenges** identified in the assessment phase. For example, if the assessment reveals a pattern of leaving due to inadequate compensation, an intervention might involve seeking additional funding sources or reallocating budgets to enhance teacher salaries. On the other hand, issues like lack of professional development could be addressed by partnering with local educational institutions to provide ongoing training and career advancement opportunities for teachers.

FOSTER A SUPPORTIVE COMMUNITY

Creating a strong sense of community among educators can be incredibly effective in reducing feelings of isolation and burnout. Directors should consider developing mentorship programs where more experienced teachers support newcomers and foster collaborative planning time so teachers can share resources and strategies. These efforts not only improve morale but also build a collective sense of purpose and belonging, critical factors in teacher retention.

INTEGRATE WORK-LIFE BALANCE PRACTICES

Promoting work-life balance is another pivotal intervention strategy. Directors can achieve this by offering flexible scheduling, considering job-sharing arrangements, or establishing protocols that respect teachers' time outside of work hours. These interventions signal to staff that their well-being is valued and that they are more than just employees; they are individuals with lives and responsibilities outside the classroom.

UPGRADE THE WORK ENVIRONMENT

Improving the physical work environment can also have a profound impact on teacher satisfaction. This might involve renovating facilities to create more pleasant and functional spaces or investing in resources and technologies that make teachers' jobs easier and more enjoyable. A splash of paint can change the entire feel of a center. Possibly make an area for a mental health break. Add a relaxing chair, some headphones with soft music, and maybe a comfy blanket. While these improvements require investment, the returns on teacher morale and retention can justify the expenditure.

IMPLEMENT REGULAR FEEDBACK LOOPS

Another crucial intervention involves establishing regular feedback loops. Teachers should feel heard and know that their opinions matter. By implementing processes for teachers to provide input on program decisions and suggest improvements, directors demonstrate a commitment to an inclusive and responsive workplace culture.

PROVIDE RECOGNITION AND ADVANCEMENT

Recognition for hard work and accomplishments can never be overstated. Whether through formal awards, acknowledgments during staff meetings, or simple notes of appreciation, recognizing teachers' efforts bolsters their motivation and job satisfaction. One of my favorites is the Glow and Grow concept. Take a blank thank you card and walk by the classroom. Peek in and observe what is being taught. Then, write a little note with what you liked, the Glow, and what can be improved, the Grow. Coupled with clear pathways for career advancement, such appreciation makes educators feel their growth and professional development are taken seriously within the organization.

ENSURE EQUITABLE POLICIES

Lastly, placing a strong emphasis on equity and inclusivity can significantly reduce staff turnover. This means creating policies and procedures that ensure all teachers and staff, regardless of background or experience level, have access to the same opportunities and resources. By doing so, a message of fairness and respect is sent throughout the organization, contributing to a culture where every teacher feels valued and supported.

In short, through precise and empathetic interventions that address the root causes of teacher attrition, directors can build a formidable framework for teacher retention. The successful implementation of such strategies relies on a continuous assessment of their effectiveness and a willingness to adapt and refine approaches based on feedback and results. This dynamic process not only stabilizes the workforce but also enhances the quality of education that programs offer to our youngest learners.

IMPROVEMENT AND STRATEGIC INTERVENTION

Understanding the root causes of teacher attrition is crucial for identifying areas for improvement and strategic intervention. By conducting a thorough assessment of the factors contributing to attrition, directors can pinpoint specific areas that require attention and develop targeted interventions to address these challenges effectively.

MOVING FORWARD WITH STRATEGIC INTERVENTIONS

Through a comprehensive analysis of the factors contributing to teacher attrition, it becomes clear that targeted interventions are necessary to address specific pain points. It's essential for directors to take proactive steps in implementing these interventions to **improve teacher retention** and cultivate a supportive environment.

UTILIZE DATA TO DRIVE DECISION-MAKING

Data-driven decision-making is a powerful tool in addressing the root causes of teacher attrition. By leveraging quantitative and qualitative data, directors can gain valuable insights into the areas that require attention, allowing them to **implement informed strategies**.

ESTABLISH SUPPORTIVE PROFESSIONAL DEVELOPMENT PROGRAMS

Investing in quality professional development programs is crucial for retaining top teaching talent. These programs should be tailored to address the specific needs and challenges faced by teachers, providing them with the tools and resources to excel in their roles.

CREATE MENTORSHIP OPPORTUNITIES

Establishing **mentorship programs** can provide new teachers with the support and guidance they need to navigate the challenges of their roles. Pairing experienced educators with new teachers can foster a supportive environment and help alleviate the feelings of isolation that often contribute to attrition.

SUPPORT WORK-LIFE BALANCE

Promoting a **healthy work-life balance** is essential for preventing burnout and retaining teachers. Directors can implement policies and practices that prioritize the well-being of their staff, ensuring that they have the support they need to thrive both personally and professionally.

FOSTER A CULTURE OF COLLABORATION AND RECOGNITION

Encouraging **collaboration** and **employee recognition** can go a long way in creating a positive and supportive work environment. When teachers feel valued and appreciated for their contributions, they are more likely to remain committed to their roles.

By addressing these critical areas with strategic interventions, directors can work towards creating a thriving, supportive environment where teacher attrition is minimized and top teaching talent is retained for the benefit of the children and the program as a whole.

CHAPTER 4

Proactive Strategies For Improving Teacher Retention

Background

The morning light barely peeked through the swaying branches of the oak tree outside the window, and Olivia was already deep in thought. She sat at a smal wooden table that seemed as ancient as time itself, her hands folded neatly atop a much-loved ledger filled with musings and strategies on early childhood education.

The challenges she faced as a director of a local preschool were far from trivial, and in the tranquility of dawn, she contemplated the delicate dance of sustaining teacher motivation and dedication.

The air around her was still, charged with the hush of an unspoken prayer for guidance. As she flipped through the pages of her ledger, her mind wandered to the vibrant collage of children's artwork that adorned the opposite wall. Each piece was a testament to the creativity and patience of her teachers. The tranquility was sporadically interrupted by the chirping of morning birds, stirring her from her reverie and reminding her that the day's toil was nigh.

She recalled a recent conversation with a cherished colleague who had breathed her fears into existence, whispering confessions of burnout and waning passion. The weight of such confidence felt heavy on Olivia's heart; losing a teacher meant disrupting the delicate fabric of her small school's culture.

A soft sigh escaped her as she recognized that a proactive approach was her strongest ally - crafting a working environment that not only addressed challenges but celebrated the triumphs and dedication of her staff. She plotted wellness initiatives, professional development opportunities, and team-building exercises, knowing that fostering a sense of community was critical.

Her focus shifted to the actionable strategies she could implement. Perhaps a mentorship program for the newer educators or a system that allowed for more fluid communication and feedback, taking lessons from past implementations that had transformed the ambiance of her staff room from a place of mere conversation to one of lively collaboration and support.

As her ledger began to brim with ideas, a soft rap at the door signaled the arrival of her assistant, the sun now cresting the horizon and bathing the room in a golden hue. It brought a semblance of warmth and a subtle reminder of the promise held in each new day. She rose, her plans still embryonic, yet she felt a growing conviction that she could indeed turn the tides on attrition, rekindling the spark that set her teachers alight with a passion for educating the youngest minds.

Olivia understood the imperativeness of her role in not just crafting curricula but nurturing the educators entrusted with its delivery. The symbiosis of satisfaction and retention, she mused, perhaps lay within the very walls of her school, in the hearts of her teachers, and the smiles of the children they taught.

In the wake of her contemplative morning, as the day's rhythm picked up the pace, she pondered—how could this proactive paradigm be woven into the very fabric of early childhood education, transcending her small school and reshaping the field at large?

UNLEASHING POTENTIAL: PROACTIVE STEPS FORWARD

Crafting a thriving educational ecosystem where early childhood educators not only start but choose to continue their career journey requires strategic foresight and action. Teacher turnover in early childhood programs has long been a source of concern, as it disrupts the continuity of care critical to a child's development and imposes significant costs on institutions. It is within this nuanced landscape that we embark on an exploration of proactive strategies designed to **retain and empower teachers**. This chapter dissects the complexities and challenges these educators face, laying a foundation on which we can build innovative and effective retention initiatives.

Firstly, we must delve into the heart of the difficulties that sap the stamina of early childhood educators. Inadequate compensation, limited professional growth opportunities, and burnout from high-stakes job demands are not mere inconveniences—they're serious, systemic issues that can erode passion and lead to attrition. Recognizing these challenges is the essential first step; life in the classroom isn't simply about a love for teaching but also about navigating a landscape peppered with constant demands and static resources. This understanding sets the stage for us to **identify precise strategies** that engage the issues head-on, transforming potential points of departure into anchors of satisfaction and growth.

The equation seems straightforward: create a positive work environment, and teachers will stay. Yet, the translation of this concept into tangible reality is far from simple. It is here that we explore how leadership can foster environments that resonate with respect, support, and shared vision. Proactive leadership, shown through consistent mentoring programs, access to professional development, and the creation of a collegial culture, doesn't just patch up retention issues temporarily—it sows the seeds for lasting satisfaction and commitment.

As readers seek actionable paths forward, this chapter doesn't merely hint at solutions but provides **concrete strategies**. From innovative mentorship models to flexible career pathways, these are not theoretical constructs but battle-tested methods gleaned from successful early childhood programs. Building on the foundation of empathy and understanding, leadership proactivity transforms into practical retention tools, which act as bulwarks against the steady tide of teacher turnover.

Evidence-based discussion navigates through the intricacies of teacher retention, backed by current research and real-world examples. This chapter leverages data to underscore the importance of each strategy, reinforcing its validity and elevating the conversation from anecdotal to analytical. The insights gained here are not ephemeral; they are deeply researched and presented with the purpose of equipping leaders with the necessary tools to enact lasting change.

In fostering an **empowering and growth-centric message**, we advocate for continuous professional development and advocate for a mindset shift toward proactive retention efforts. By adopting a collaborative spirit, we encourage educational leaders to cultivate dialogue and inclusivity, embracing diverse perspectives and experiences that reflect our broader society. The support structures that we propose do more than help teachers stick around—they help them thrive and, in turn, magnify their impact on the youngest and most impressionable among us.

To encapsulate, this chapter is a commitment to action over resignation, a decisive step towards empowerment over attrition. It's a blueprint for leaders who are ready to acknowledge challenges, reimagine their approach, and **forge a new path** where teachers not only start but choose to stay, grow, and lead.

In the fast-paced and demanding world of early childhood education, teachers face unique challenges that can significantly impact retention rates. From long hours and heavy workloads to emotional strain and low salaries, the early childhood education field presents obstacles that contribute to high turnover. It's important to recognize these challenges and understand that proactive strategies can be implemented to address the underlying factors contributing to attrition. In order to retain top teaching talent, it's crucial to take a proactive approach, fostering a positive working environment that promotes teacher retention and satisfaction.

One of the key challenges that early childhood educators face is the **emotional strain** that comes with nurturing and educating young children. The need for emotional resilience and patience cannot be understated in this field. Additionally, the demanding nature of the job can lead to burnout, impacting a teacher's sense of wellbeing and job satisfaction. It's imperative to acknowledge the emotional challenges early childhood educators face and proactively provide them with support and resources to maintain their emotional wellbeing.

Another significant challenge is the modest compensation and limited professional growth opportunities in the early childhood education field, which can contribute to high turnover rates. Early childhood teachers often receive lower salaries compared to their counterparts in elementary and secondary education. This pay disparity can lead to frustration and dissatisfaction, prompting educators to seek opportunities in other sectors. To address this issue proactively, it's crucial to advocate for fair compensation and create pathways for professional growth and development within the field.

Bell (2021) wrote a summary of the critical issue of early teacher turnover and the problems of being unable to pay teachers a livable wage. In an interview with Cindy Owens, New Testament Child Development Center director and owner in Union County, Owens stated that in her area, "even fast food (restaurants) are doing sign-on bonuses" (p. 2) and that she had not always paid herself in order to pay her staff. Owens mentioned that many of her teachers live on government assistance. Owens indicated, "I think many people who make the laws and the standards do not realize what level of folks are living" (p. 3).

In another investigation, Researcher Bullough et al. (2012) conducted a study with 89 Head Start teachers, teacher assistants, and classroom aides to learn more about Head Start and the implications of the increased teaching qualifications.

As a result, they found that most participants enjoyed their jobs; however, they commonly shared that they were unhappy with the pay level.Several teachers indicated they are passionate about serving children and feel they are giving back to the community.However, while teaching staff enjoy their jobs,many struggle

financially. In the survey, they were asked if they had considered leaving Head Start, and 58% of the respondents indicated they had. Other variables for leaving included career change, dissatisfaction with past leadership, stress, and more. Forty percent of the participants also "included financial issues as among their greatest worries, disappointments, or drawbacks related to working with Head Start" (p. 3). Bullough et al. (2012) also found that the increase in Head Start teaching qualifications makes hiring and retaining credentialed staff with low pay more difficult. Many of the young, credentialed teachers responded that they do not intend to stay teaching in the program.

Furthermore, maintaining a work-life balance can be particularly challenging for early childhood educators due to the demanding nature of the job. Long hours, extensive lesson planning, and administrative responsibilities can encroach on personal time, leading to stress and fatigue. Proactive measures such as implementing effective time management strategies, flexible scheduling, and workload support can greatly contribute to a healthier work-life balance for teachers.

In addition, unique regulatory requirements and administrative responsibilities in the early childhood education field can add to the challenges teachers face. Navigating complex state regulations, curriculum standards, and assessment requirements requires a considerable amount of time and effort. By providing educators with the necessary support, guidance, and resources to manage these responsibilities proactively, the burden can be alleviated, contributing to a positive work environment.

Understanding and addressing these challenges proactively is essential for promoting teacher retention and satisfaction. It's important to recognize that by taking proactive measures to address these factors, a positive working environment can be cultivated, one that supports and values the contributions of early childhood educators.

Understanding how proactive measures can lead to a positive working environment that promotes teacher retention and satisfaction is crucial for educators and administrators in the early childhood education field; by proactively addressing the challenges that lead to high turnover rates, a supportive and thriving work environment can be cultivated. **This not only benefits the teachers but also positively impacts the quality of education provided to the children in their care**. Let's explore how proactive strategies can lay the foundation for a positive and nurturing workplace

Creating a positive working environment begins with addressing the underlying factors contributing to high turnover rates among early childhood educators. **By recognizing and addressing challenges such as low pay, lack of professional development opportunities, and high-stress levels**, proactive measures can be implemented to mitigate these issues. Rather than waiting for problems to escalate, the focus shifts to prevention and proactive solutions to create a supportive and rewarding work environment. **This shift in approach sets the stage for attracting and retaining top teaching talent** in the early childhood education field.

When proactive measures are in place, the work environment becomes a place where educators feel supported and valued. **Investing in ongoing professional development and mentorship opportunities** helps teachers feel that they are continuing to grow and improve in their roles. This not only enhances their skill set but also boosts their confidence and job satisfaction. Furthermore, providing **clear communication, feedback, and recognition** for their efforts reinforces a culture of support and appreciation, which is a hallmark of a positive work environment.

Positive working environments are known to foster collaboration and a sense of community. When teachers feel connected to their colleagues and the leadership team, they are more likely to remain in their positions. This sense of community provides a network of support, encouragement, and resource-sharing that can make a significant difference in teacher retention. As a result, educators are more likely to feel satisfied and fulfilled in their roles when they have a network of peers and mentors who understand and support their work.

Moreover, creating a positive work environment through proactive measures can lead to an increase in overall job satisfaction. **When educators feel that their well-being is valued and their needs are being met**, they are more likely to experience higher job satisfaction. This satisfaction is not only beneficial for individual teachers but also has a ripple effect, positively impacting the overall morale and atmosphere of the entire early childhood education program.

By understanding how proactive measures can lead to a positive working environment that promotes teacher retention and satisfaction, early childhood educators and program administrators can implement targeted strategies to create a supportive and thriving workplace. Recognizing and addressing the challenges that lead to high turnover rates, investing in ongoing professional development, fostering a sense of community, and prioritizing job satisfaction are all critical components of this proactive approach. **In doing so, a positive and nurturing workplace can be established, benefitting both educators and the children in their care.**

STEPS FORWARD

INVEST IN PROFESSIONAL DEVELOPMENT

A central pillar for bolstering teacher retention is a robust **professional development** program. Continuous learning opportunities are not only essential for enhancing teaching skills but also serve to convey to educators that their personal growth is valued. A culture of ongoing learning within your early childhood education program can significantly influence teachers' decisions to stay on board. To implement this, offer regular workshops, provide access to online courses, and arrange peer mentoring programs. These initiatives empower teachers with new strategies and techniques, keeping them intellectually stimulated and professionally fulfilled.

MENTORSHIP: A TWO-FOLD BENEFIT

Mentorship programs can be particularly transformative. Pairing new or less experienced teachers with veteran mentors creates an environment of support and shared knowledge. Beyond the immediate practical benefits, such programs foster a sense of belonging and community. The more experienced teachers often find renewed purpose in guiding their colleagues, while the mentees gain invaluable insights and a reassuring support network. This mutual exchange not only enhances efficacy in the classroom but also roots teachers in the institution, reducing the likelihood of turnover.

RETOOLING THE WORK ENVIRONMENT

Adaptable work conditions are another key strategy for retaining teachers. Conduct surveys to understand the needs and preferences of your staff, and consider options like flexible scheduling or job-sharing arrangements. Creating an environment where teachers feel that their life outside of work is respected can heighten job satisfaction and loyalty. Simple changes in scheduling or allowing for more autonomy in the classroom can lead to substantial improvements in a teacher's sense of agency and work-life balance.

COMPETITIVE COMPENSATION

Despite often tight budgets, **competitive pay** and **benefits** are critical for retention. Monitor industry standards to ensure that your compensation packages are on par with or exceed those of similar institutions. Where possible, sweeten the deal with bonuses for tenure, exceptional performance, or added responsibilities. Benefits such as comprehensive health care, retirement plans, and tuition assistance for further education can also be significant factors in a teacher's length of service.

CREATE A COMMUNITY OF PRACTICE

Fostering a **community of practice** is instrumental in building a collaborative and supportive teaching environment. Establishing regular team meetings for educators to share ideas, resources, and challenges promotes collegiality and a unified mission. Within this collective, teachers can develop a shared repertoire of resources: experiences, stories, tools, and ways of addressing recurring problems. This sense of community and shared purpose is a powerful antidote to the isolation that can drive teachers away from the field.

ACKNOWLEDGE AND REWARD DEDICATION

Never underestimate the power of **recognition**. Regularly acknowledge the hard work and dedication of your teachers through awards, public appreciation, or even a simple 'thank you.' These gestures reinforce the value of each educator's contribution and solidify their commitment to the program. Teachers who feel recognized are more likely to invest deeply in their roles, resulting in heightened job satisfaction and decreased turnover rates.

ENCOURAGE TEACHER LEADERSHIP

Inviting teachers to take on **leadership roles** within the program can also serve as a vital retention tool. Leadership roles can vary from spearheading a new teaching initiative to representing the school in the community or professional organizations. These opportunities can provide a stimulating challenge and can help a teacher feel more deeply connected to the success of the program. By engaging in leadership, teachers can affect change and innovation, which not only enriches the learning environment but also enhances their own professional narrative.

GATHER AND ACT ON FEEDBACK

Lastly, promoting open communication and acting on teacher feedback demonstrates that their voices are heard and respected. Implement regular feedback mechanisms, such as suggestion boxes or staff surveys, and, most importantly, show that you take their input seriously by addressing concerns and exploring suggested improvements. When teachers see the tangible effects of their feedback, they are reassured that the program is dynamic and responsive, making them more likely to remain loyal and engaged.

In summary, it is evident that **proactive measures** play a crucial role in improving teacher retention in the early childhood education field. By recognizing the **unique challenges** faced by early childhood educators, we can implement strategies to address them head-on. This approach not only **promotes teacher satisfaction** but also creates a positive working environment that fosters retention.

Understanding the tangible benefits of proactive measures is essential. Through the implementation of **actionable strategies**, we can enhance teacher retention in the early childhood education field. Moreover, these strategies have the potential to transform the landscape of early childhood education, leading to a more sustainable and thriving workforce.

Ultimately, the proactive approach to improving teacher retention offers hope and potential for positive change in the field of early childhood education. As we move forward, it is crucial to remember that **our efforts** have a direct impact on the retention and satisfaction of teachers and, by extension, on the quality of education and care provided to young children.

CHAPTER 5

Embracing Diverse Perspectives On Teacher Retention

Background

The first light of dawn barely pierced through the heavy morning mist, casting long shadows on the playground of the Head Start program where Claire, the director, stood contemplating the quiet before the day's storm of activity. She inhaled deeply, the air crisp with the scent of dew on the grass, mingling with the distant aroma of the cafeteria's brewing coffee. She knew in a few hours, the grounds would be filled with the laughter and energy of children, but for now, it was her refuge to ponder the weighty problem that had settled on her shoulders like an unwelcome winter coat.

She considered the mosaic of her staff, a rich tapestry of different cultures, experiences, and insights – each one a potentially crucial piece in solving the puzzle of retention. How to weave these strands together into a durable solution? Claire's experiences underscored the importance of job satisfaction, competitive compensation, and a potent mix of professional development and supportive leadership, but translating theory into practice was like trying to catch the mist in her hands – seemingly simple, yet impossibly complex.

The breeze rustled the leaves, bringing her thoughts back to the physical world and reminding her of the workshop she had attended last summer. The ideas presented there, focusing on transformational leadership and embracing diverse perspectives for a more holistic strategy, resonated deeply. Could the key lie not in individual solutions but in the synthesis of them all? As her mind charted pathways to weave these threads into a new strategy, she felt a cautious optimism bloom amidst the doubt.

A soft giggle broke through the morning calm, and she turned to see early arrivals scampering to the playground. Their innocent joy grounded her, reminding her why she was doing this: for every child's chance at a Head Start, for every teacher's need to be heard and valued, for a community's vibrancy hinged on the success of this program. The problem was multifaceted, but so was the solution – a vision of a vibrant, sustainable ecosystem began to take form in her mind.

The children's playful shouts and a teacher's warm greeting in the near distance stitched a fabric of normalcy around her. But the needle of change was in Claire's hand, and the thread was composed of diverse perspectives, shared goals, and collective change. As the day unfolded before her, with its share of smiles and challenges, Claire mulled over one final piece of the complex puzzle: How might a community's embrace of a comprehensive framework for teacher retention become the cornerstone for the flourishing of its youngest and most vulnerable members?

THE MULTIFACETED PUZZLE OF TEACHER RETENTION

On the ever-evolving landscape of early childhood education, **teacher retention** stands as one of the most pressing challenges confronting early childhood programs across the nation. Persistent attrition not only affects the stability of our classrooms but also undermines the quality of care and education that we strive to provide for our youngest learners. Yet, the solution to this conundrum isn't found in a one-size-fits-all approach but in a rich tapestry woven from diverse perspectives. This chapter embarks on a journey to uncover the multifarious factors influencing teacher retention, highlighting the indispensable role of a diverse, holistic approach in creating environments where educators thrive.

Transforming teacher retention demands that we first understand the myriad **sources of job** satisfaction. What compels a teacher to stay in a position, and on the contrary, what drives them to leave? It is by nurturing job satisfaction that we fortify the pillars on which teacher retention stands. Compensation, surely a significant component, must be considered alongside professional development opportunities and the influence of transformational leadership. These elements operate in concert, each as crucial as the next in fostering a climate where early childhood professionals feel valued, supported, and motivated.

Next, we delve into the importance of amalgamating multiple perspectives in the quest to enhance **leadership support**. Empowering leaders within early childhood programs isn't a task relegated to chance; it involves a deliberate cultivation of talent and an unwavering commitment to professional growth. When directors and administrators employ a panoramic lens to view teacher retention — one that appreciates the intricate interplay between individual needs and organizational goals — they set the stage for a new era of educational excellence.

Unlocking the potential of our educators also requires a keen understanding of how to leverage the rich experiences found within our own communities. It is not enough to craft policies from the top down; we must engage in a dialogue with those on the front lines, co-creating strategies that reflect a deep respect for their unique insights and expertise. As readers move through the forthcoming sections, they will gain the tools not only to identify but also to implement strategies that encourage longevity, foster satisfaction, and, ultimately, reduce the rate of teacher turnover.

With a clear **goal** to transform early childhood programs through enhanced teacher retention and leadership support, this chapter presents a step-by-step process for one of the most effective strategies available: developing a robust mentorship program. To do so, it is vital to embark on a structured journey that begins with mobilizing current educators as mentors and culminates in a culture of mutual growth and professional fulfillment.

CRAFTING CONNECTION: A MENTORSHIP MAP FOR TEACHER EXCELLENCE

STEP 1: IDENTIFY POTENTIAL MENTORS

Before the mentorship seeds can grow, they must first be sowed. Seeking out tenured educators with a knack for leadership and communication lays the groundwork for a mentorship network. Ask, who among the staff embodies the spirit of early childhood and exhibits potential as a beacon for new teachers?

STEP 2: ASSIGN MENTORS TO NEW TEACHERS

The alignment of teaching styles and personalities can turn a good mentor-mentee pair into a great one. Facilitating these partnerships ensures that new teachers are not just surviving but truly thriving through personalized guidance and support.

STEP 3: PROVIDE MENTOR TRAINING

To build a sturdy bridge between new and experienced teachers, mentors must be given the right tools. Training that focuses on active listening, feedback delivery, and program navigation transforms well-intentioned educators into adept mentors.

STEP 4: ESTABLISH REGULAR MENTOR-MENTEE MEETINGS

Consistency is the golden thread in the mentorship tapestry, creating time and space for shared experiences. It is through these regular interactions that trust is built and professional development is nurtured.

STEP 5: FOSTER COLLABORATION AND PROFESSIONAL GROWTH

The heart of mentorship lies in collective growth. Encouraging joint lesson planning and attendance at professional events further solidifies the mentor-mentee relationship while cementing a culture of collegiality and lifelong learning.

STEP 6: EVALUATE AND ADJUST THE MENTORSHIP PROGRAM

Reflection is a key component of successful mentorship programs. Regular evaluations enable the program to adapt and evolve, ensuring it remains responsive to the needs of new teachers and aligns with the broader objectives of the organization.

STEP 7: RECOGNIZE AND REWARD MENTORS

Gratitude and recognition are not only courteous but imperative. Acknowledging the efforts of mentors not only elevates their morale but also showcases the value of their indispensable contributions to the entire early childhood community.

By following this blueprint, early childhood programs can foster a learning environment that not only supports teachers through their initial steps but also elevates them throughout their journey. Engaging with the rich array of perspectives and experiences that exist among educators can transform the challenges of teacher retention into opportunities for collaborative growth and leadership development. Through the proposed mentorship program and the strategies outlined, we invite early childhood programs to not just imagine a more sustainable future — it is within grasp.

Teacher retention and leadership support are complex issues that require a comprehensive and multifaceted approach. To truly understand the scope of these challenges, it is crucial to embrace diverse perspectives that encompass the many contributing factors to attrition. By integrating a wide range of viewpoints, we can gain a more nuanced understanding of the issues at hand and develop effective strategies to improve teacher retention rates and leadership support.

One key benefit of embracing diverse perspectives is the opportunity to gain a more holistic understanding of the challenges surrounding teacher retention. **By considering the experiences and insights of teachers from different backgrounds, we can uncover unique factors that contribute to attrition**. This can include the impact of culture, family dynamics, and community factors, all of which can play a significant role in a teacher's decision to stay or leave their position. Without considering these diverse perspectives, we may miss out on crucial insights that could inform our retention strategies.

Moreover, embracing diverse perspectives enables us to address the issue of leadership support in a more comprehensive manner. **By engaging with the perspectives of directors, administrators, and other educational leaders, we can gain a clearer picture of the challenges they face in supporting and retaining their teaching staff.** This can include insights into resource allocation, professional development opportunities, and the impact of administrative practices on staff morale. By taking these diverse viewpoints into account, we can develop more effective strategies to support leadership in creating a positive and sustainable work environment.

Another important aspect of embracing diverse perspectives is the opportunity to consider the influence of external factors on teacher retention and leadership support. **By engaging with research, data, and expert opinions, we can gain a deeper understanding of the systemic issues that contribute to attrition in early childhood education**. This can include issues related to compensation, career advancement opportunities, and the overall status of the early childhood education profession. By integrating these diverse sources of information, we can develop a more comprehensive framework for addressing these challenges.

In summary, embracing diverse perspectives is crucial for gaining a comprehensive understanding of teacher retention and leadership support in early childhood programs. By considering the experiences of teachers, leaders, and experts from a wide range of backgrounds, we can develop more effective strategies to improve retention rates and create a supportive and thriving environment for both teachers and students.

CHAPTER 6

Cultivating A Supportive Workplace Culture

Background

The morning sun cast a glow across the classroom, dust particles floating like idle thoughts in a ray of light. Thomas stood before an arrangement of empty centers, contemplating the fledgling day nestled in the heart of spring. The stillness of the room belied the storm of concerns that unfurled in his mind. Today, he would initiate a mentorship program for his fellow educators, a step towards curating the kind of supportive atmosphere that he knew was crucial for their collective fulfillment.

He recalled a seminar he'd attended, where the speaker had underlined the significance of an inclusive workplace culture and how it wasn't just a matter of policy but the thread that could weave a community together or fray it irreparably. With a deep breath, Thomas began pinning his ideas to the corkboard, the sharp tap of the pins anchoring his resolve.

A colleague, Sarah, drifted into the room, her smile a soft reminder of camaraderie. Their exchange was brief, a shared acknowledgment of the challenge ahead. She, too, believed in the transformational power of unity, of open dialogue that allowed every voice to find its tenor in the symphony of school affairs.

The chatter of students began to fill the halls, a cacophony of youth and promise. Thomas smiled, their energy infections, a reminder of why he'd chosen this path. As they entered, Thomas greeted each one, recognizing the impact his mood had on the room—the ripple effect of positivity that starts with a single, genuine interaction.

Lunchtime found him in the break room with fellow teachers, discussing how collaborative decision-making might elevate their sense of agency at school. Some were skeptical, scarred by bureaucracy, and worn by lack of recognition, but Thomas was unwavering in his belief that together, they could engender change. He spoke of studies showing how empowered teachers led to lively classrooms and improved student outcomes, his words not just a plea for solidarity but a roadmap to rejuvenation.

The day wound on, ebbing like a tide as Thomas stood at the window, the orange hues of sunset washing over his face. Had he made a difference today? The seed was planted, but would it take root in the fertile ground of communal hope or wither in the shadow of systemic inertia?

He pondered upon the indelible link between supportive work culture and teacher retention—how the echo of acknowledgment could keep a good educator anchored to a school, to a community. Would his colleagues eschew the comfort of the status quo for the uncharted path of unity and shared-growth he proposed?

What will it take for the importance of fostering such a culture to become more than just an ideal but a living, breathing paradigm in the fabric of educational institutions?

FROM SEEDS TO ORCHARDS: GROWING THE WORK CULTURE THAT NURTURES

Unlocking the full potential of any organization hinges on the wellness and engagement of its workforce. In the sphere of early childhood education, where the turnover of dedicated staff can ripple across the lives of countless children, nurturing a supportive workplace culture isn't just about job satisfaction—it's about securing a brighter future for the youngest learners. In the journey to transform early childhood programs, steering the ship requires more than just navigating challenges; it involves fostering an environment where teachers can thrive.

The cornerstone of a flourishing educational program lies in its ability to retain dedicated professionals committed to nurturing young minds. A supportive and inclusive culture in the workplace extends beyond the surface-level satisfaction of employees—it's about instilling a sense of belonging and purpose.

Efforts that prioritize effective communication, mentorship, and collaborative decision-making not only cement a teacher's loyalty to an institution but also deepen their commitment to the integral work they perform. Here, we unveil the stratagem that empowers early childhood leaders to cultivate a greenhouse for growth, even when contending with the traditional constraints of resources and support.

Every teacher enters the profession with a unique set of aspirations and challenges. Acknowledging this diversity is the first step toward building an inclusive culture that values individual contributions while steering the collective toward shared goals. This chapter will guide readers through understanding the imperative of fostering such a culture, learning the tools to build it, and recognizing its profound impact on teacher retention and satisfaction.

THE FOUNDATIONS OF EFFECTIVE COMMUNICATION

At its nucleus, effective communication catalyzes mutual trust and understanding, laying the groundwork for a supportive workplace. It is imperative for leaders to foster an environment where open dialogue flourishes and where teachers feel both seen and heard. The exchange of candid feedback and the active engagement of educators in decision-making processes not only bolsters morale but also enhances the sense of ownership and accountability within the team.

MENTORSHIP: THE LIGHTHOUSE AMIDST ROUGH SEAS

As previously discussed in chapter 5, a well-structured mentorship program is instrumental for onboarding new educators and providing them with an anchor in the often turbulent seas of early childhood education. Seasoned teachers carry a torch of wisdom that, when shared, can illuminate the path for newcomers. In turn, experienced educators are revitalized through the fresh perspectives and energy of their mentees, crafting a symbiotic relationship that strengthens the fabric of the institution.

COALESCING IN DECISION MAKING

Empowering teachers to have a voice in decisions that affect their classrooms and professional development crystallizes a sense of shared leadership. This collaborative stance not only enriches the decision-making process with a multiplicity of insights but also upholds a democratic and respectful workplace ethos. It echoes the message that every member's viewpoint is not only welcomed but also deemed essential to the collective's success.

In synthesizing a culture that embraces these elements, early childhood programs can transform an industry often riddled with turnover into a beacon of steadfastness and commitment. As we delve into the tactical approach to building, you will find that the trajectory of teacher retention and satisfaction can indeed be shaped by the culture fostered within the workplace.

PLANTING THE STEPS FOR GROWTH – PROFESSIONAL DEVELOPMENT PLANS

STEP 1: ASSESS TEACHERS' NEEDS AND GOALS

The construction of individualized frameworks begins with a careful assessment of the diverse landscapes each educator tills. Through self-reflection and constructive conversations, leaders and teachers together uncover the soil's strengths and the nutrients it lacks. Achieving this requires an appreciation for the multifaceted nature of teaching—a union of art and science, of personal connection and pedagogical expertise.

STEP 2: PROMOTE GOAL-SETTING

In setting objectives, the SMART goal criteria serve as the gardener's stakes and strings, providing direction and form. Teachers, with the guidance of their leaders, plant seeds for objectives that are both challenging and attainable, catering to both the teacher's personal growth and the overarching mission of the program.

According to MindTools.com, SMART goals allow you to write goals that are clear, attainable, and meaningful.

S – specific
M - measurable
A - achievable
R - relevant
T – time-bound

STEP 3: IDENTIFY PROFESSIONAL DEVELOPMENT OPPORTUNITIES

Like selecting the optimal environment for a seedling, linking teachers with the right opportunities and resources can make the critical difference between stagnation and flourishing. An array of professional growth options ensures that all educators find the training and mentorship that resonate with their personalized path and the necessities of the classroom.

STEP 4: CREATE A TIMELINE AND ACTION PLAN

With a clear plan mapping out the key waypoints, teachers can chart their journey of growth with both flexibility and structure. Such a timeline acts as the trellis guiding the growth upwards—visible, tangible, and adaptable.

STEP 5: SUPPORT IMPLEMENTATION AND REFLECTION

Real growth occurs in the nurturing phase—teachers actively engage with their newfound knowledge, and leaders foster a reflective culture where learning is applied and adapted. Having limbs reach out for light and water, educators incorporate new strategies and insights into their daily practice.

STEP 6: MONITOR PROGRESS AND PROVIDE FEEDBACK

Regular checkpoints for evaluation and feedback keep the developmental process attuned and responsive. Such monitoring ensures that while reaching for the sky, the growth remains firm and directed, not straying from its intended path.

STEP 7: EVALUATE AND ADJUST

Just as ecosystems evolve, so too must the professional development approach, adapting and evolving through continuous assessment. The dynamic nature of the educational field demands that leadership remains agile, ready to prune or support as the landscape shifts.

STEP 8: CELEBRATE ACHIEVEMENTS

Recognizing and celebrating the milestones, big and small, not only bolsters morale but also cements the sense of accomplishment and progress. This fosters a culture of acknowledgment and appreciation, encouraging further growth and dedication.

In fostering these roots of development, early childhood programs can not only invigorate their workforce but also fortify the foundations upon which young learners will build their future.

Building a positive and inclusive workplace culture is crucial for ensuring the satisfaction and retention of teachers within an early childhood program. When teachers feel supported, valued, and included, they are more likely to stay in their roles and contribute to the success of the program. A positive workplace culture fosters a sense of belonging, encourages collaboration, and promotes professional growth, all of which are essential for the well-being of educators and the continuity of quality care and education for children.

Effective communication is a cornerstone of a supportive workplace culture. When leadership and management communicate openly and transparently with teachers, it creates an environment of trust and respect. Teachers feel empowered when they are kept informed about program decisions, changes, and developments. Open communication also encourages teachers to share their ideas, concerns, and feedback, leading to a more collaborative and inclusive work environment.

Mentorship programs play a crucial role in providing support and guidance to new and existing teachers. Pairing experienced educators with newer staff members allows for the exchange of knowledge, skills, and best practices. This collaborative approach not only enhances the professional development of teachers but also creates a sense of community and support within the program.

Collaborative decision-making further contributes to a supportive workplace culture. When teachers are included in important decisions that affect their work and the overall program, they feel valued and respected. Involving teachers in the decision-making process also leads to better solutions, as it harnesses the collective wisdom and experience of the entire team.

Cultivating a supportive and inclusive workplace culture is not just beneficial for the individual teacher, but it ultimately leads to improved teacher satisfaction and retention, benefiting the program as a whole. It is important to acknowledge the impact a positive workplace culture can have on the well-being of both teachers and students, as well as the overall quality of the educational experience.

As we delve further into the strategies and benefits of cultivating a supportive workplace culture, we will explore how these elements contribute to teacher satisfaction and retention, providing actionable insights for your program's success.

Effective communication, mentorship programs, and collaborative decision-making are crucial tools for building a supportive work environment in any educational setting. **Clear and transparent communication** is the cornerstone of a healthy workplace culture, as it facilitates understanding, trust, and collaboration among teachers and administrators. When information flows freely and openly, it fosters a sense of inclusion and involvement, allowing teachers to feel valued and heard. Open lines of communication also enable teachers to express their needs and concerns, creating a collaborative environment where everyone feels supported and empowered.

Mentorship programs play a pivotal role in nurturing and developing the skills and well-being of teachers. **Pairing experienced educators with newer teachers** allows for the exchange of knowledge, guidance, and support. Mentors can provide valuable insights and advice, helping new teachers navigate the complexities of the educational landscape. Moreover, mentorship programs can help build a sense of community and camaraderie among staff, contributing to a supportive and cohesive work environment. When teachers feel that they have a mentor who genuinely cares about their growth and success, they are more likely to find fulfillment and purpose in their roles.

Collaborative decision-making is another powerful tool for cultivating a supportive workplace culture. **Involving teachers in the decision-making process** empowers them to take ownership of their work and creates a sense of investment in the organization. When teachers have a voice in shaping policies, curriculum, and other important aspects of the educational institution, they feel valued and respected. This participatory approach fosters a strong sense of community and camaraderie among staff, which is essential for creating a supportive and inclusive work environment.

By embracing effective communication, mentorship programs, and collaborative decision-making, educational leaders can lay the foundation for a positive and supportive workplace culture. These tools not only contribute to teacher satisfaction but also enhance retention rates. When teachers feel supported, valued, and empowered, they are more likely to stay engaged and committed to their roles, leading to improved overall retention within the organization.

Ultimately, these tools are not only essential for building a supportive work environment but also for ensuring the long-term success and sustainability of an educational institution. By fostering a culture of open communication, mentorship, and collaboration, leaders can create an environment where teachers thrive, students receive a high-quality education, and the organization as a whole can flourish.

THE SUPPORTIVE CULTURE FRAMEWORK (SCF)

The vitality of a supportive workplace culture in early childhood education cannot be overstated. Embodied in the Supportive Culture Framework (SCF), this conceptual model in systems theory delineates the nuances of nurturing environments that foster sustained teacher satisfaction and retention. The SCF framework offers early childhood directors the tools for understanding the intricate interplay among various components vital for creating a thriving educational setting.

INPUTS

Inputs are the foundational elements that flow into our system. They encompass funding, resources, policies, and regulations that set the stage for operational possibilities within programs. Think of inputs as the raw materials served up to construct the environment we desire. The quality, consistency, and relevance of these inputs directly influence the caliber of our processes and the effectiveness of our outputs. Managing these inputs vigorously means advocating for sufficient funding, sourcing appropriate resources, streamlining policies, and aligning with regulations—all pivotal to building a bedrock for sustaining teachers and supporting leadership.

PROCESSES

Processes are the mechanisms through which inputs are transformed into outputs. They include hiring practices, onboarding, professional development, and communication channels—all requiring thoughtful execution. For instance, robust hiring processes that are fair and inclusive can set the initial stage for a supportive culture. A well-structured onboarding process ensures a warm welcome and functional integration for new teachers. Regular, meaningful professional development keeps the teaching spirit ignited and growing. Transparent communication channels reduce misunderstandings and foster a sense of community. The smooth operation of these processes ensures our human assets—teachers—are well-supported and poised to succeed.

OUTPUTS

The outputs of the SCF are visible in the increased retention rates, job satisfaction levels, quality of leadership support, and, ultimately, outcomes for children. These variables are interdependent; improved teacher retention often correlates with higher job satisfaction, which in turn drives better child outcomes. Conversely, effective leadership support tends to fuel teacher growth and satisfaction, cascading into positive educational experiences for children. Measuring these outputs gives us tangible evidence of the effectiveness of our inputs and processes, prompting us to either maintain our course or make necessary adjustments.

FEEDBACK LOOPS

In any dynamic system, feedback loops allow outcomes to inform and shape the system's inputs and processes. The SCF illustrates these loops, emphasizing the importance of responsiveness. Feedback can come from teacher surveys, retention statistics, parent and child feedback, or even community engagement levels. This continuous loop of evaluation and adjustment ensures the system's relevance and effectiveness over time. Directors who actively listen to feedback and make informed changes demonstrate adaptability and a commitment to excellence.

APPLYING THE SCF IN PRACTICE

When directors implement the Supportive Culture Framework, they become architects of an environment where teachers feel valued, and students thrive. It starts with securing and managing robust inputs, then meticulously crafting processes that respect and enhance these resources. The fruits of these labors—our outputs—will speak volumes about the health and efficacy of our program. Through attentive feedback loops, we secure the pulse of our system, ready to make those incremental improvements that translate into long-lasting impacts.

In a practical context, a director might leverage the framework to pinpoint areas needing attention—perhaps onboarding programs that could include mentorship opportunities or professional development sessions that enable teachers to explore innovative teaching methods. Such targeted initiatives demonstrate the director's commitment to their team's professional growth, directly contributing to a supportive school culture.

Time and Change: Dynamics within the SCF

The stability of an early childhood education program hinges upon its ability to maintain equilibrium in the face of change—whether that's educational trends, policy shifts, or economic fluctuations. The SCF provides a scaffold for understanding how to adapt to these changes while preserving core values and objectives. By acknowledging the fluid nature of education and remaining vigilant to the needs and feedback of teachers, directors can use this model to maintain a resilient educational environment.

In conclusion, cultivating a supportive workplace culture is not a one-time event but a recurring process of assessment and adjustment. The Supportive Culture Framework offers a blueprint for understanding the complex relationships within educational settings and a pathway toward heightened teacher satisfaction and retention. By harnessing the SCF, we forge ahead in creating an ecosystem where every teacher has the support to flourish, every leader has the resources to empower, and every child has the opportunity to reach their full potential.

In cultivating a supportive workplace culture, it is evident that the commitment to fostering a positive and inclusive environment has a direct impact on teacher satisfaction and retention. **Effective communication, mentorship programs, and collaborative decision-making** have emerged as powerful tools for achieving this goal. By prioritizing these elements, early childhood leaders can actively contribute to a thriving work culture that supports the professional and personal growth of their educators.

The significance of a supportive workplace culture cannot be overstated. Research consistently demonstrates that a **positive work environment** directly correlates with higher teacher retention rates and increased job satisfaction. When teachers feel valued, heard, and supported, they are more likely to remain with the organization and fully invest in their roles. This, in turn, leads to better outcomes for the children in their care and contributes to the overall success of the program.

As we move forward, it's important for early childhood leaders to recognize that their commitment to cultivating a positive workplace culture goes beyond merely checking a box. It is a continual, multifaceted effort that involves proactive communication, ongoing mentorship, and a genuine dedication to collaborative decision-making. Embracing this approach not only enhances the well-being of teachers but also fortifies the foundation of the entire program, creating a more cohesive and effective learning environment for both educators and children.

In the next chapter, we will explore the crucial role of professional development in supporting teacher growth and retention, providing actionable strategies for empowering educators to continually improve their skills and knowledge.

CHAPTER 7

PRIORITIZING PROFESSIONAL DEVELOPMENT AND GROWTH OPPORTUNITIES

BACKGROUND

Under the watchful eye of a cloudless sky, Ms. Roxann perused her student's assessments with an expression of mingling concern and determination. The stillness of her classroom, usually brimming with the kinetic energy of youthful discovery, was a stark contrast – an empty orchestra pit awaiting the nighttime concerto. Her mind wandered not to the looming pile of anecdotal notes but rather to the untapped potential student.

Ms. Roxann had always believed in the transformational power of learning, not just for her students but for herself as an educator. She had seen firsthand the positive ripples that flowed from her colleagues who had embarked on journeys of professional development. Conversations in the teachers' lounge had often revolved around the latest pedagogical strategies or engaging workshops that challenged their paradigms, fueling a collective desire for growth.

Yet, the current silence was a canvas for reflection on her own career trajectory. It had been three years since her last professional training, and she felt the weight of stagnation. A study she had come across recently echoed through her thoughts, suggesting a direct correlation between continuous professional development and teacher satisfaction – a mirror held up to show a stark reality.

The scent of a dry-erase marker pulled her back, a reminder of the old, dependable methods she used. "How can we dance with change if our feet are mired in tradition?" she murmured. The aroma mingled with the hint of oak that wafted from her creaky desk, a nexus of a thousand lesson plans, and the silent witness to her relentless toil.

Knowing the critical impact that investing in one's own professional horizon held, Ms. Roxann resolved that action was the catalyst needed to transform her career's potential energy into kinetic momentum. Her mind buzzed with the planning of actionable strategies that would ignite a spark not only in her classroom but also within the landscape of her career. Could it be a specialized certification or perhaps a leadership role in curriculum development? Her heart raced with the possibility.

Ms. Roxann turned off her computer, the hum of the fluorescent lights overhead offering a subtle yet insistent reminder of time's passage. She envisions herself presenting at a teacher's conference, imparting newfound wisdom gleaned from bold ventures into her professional development. With a renewed sense of purpose, she contemplates how many others like her have felt the pull of potential unfulfilled. And then, the pivot: If Ms. Roxann dared to reach new heights of expertise, how might her evolution inspire those around her, from peers to pupils, spurring a renaissance borne on the wings of shared growth?

What might be the catalyst that transforms the dormant desire for progress into the palpable reality of change?

UNLEASHING POTENTIAL: THE ART OF NURTURING TEACHERS

Investing in the professional growth of teachers is not just a nicety; it's a necessity. In the complex field of early childhood education, where teacher turnover can disrupt the learning environment and impede student progress, prioritizing professional development and growth opportunities emerges as a steadfast solution. This investment is a concrete expression of commitment to the educators who shape young minds and can lead to a stable, enriched learning context for children. Understanding the significant role that professional advancement plays in job satisfaction is essential in crafting an environment where educators are not just present but engaged and progressing.

The early childhood education standards, curriculum, and increased emphasis on accountability are all changing quickly. Haslip and Gullo (2017) looked at how these changes are affecting professional development. They examined "the landscape of early childhood education is rapidly changing... driven by positive and negative trends" (p. 250). Financial support is lacking in the early childhood sector to sustain the rapidly changing early childhood landscape in areas such as in-service and pre-service teacher preparation, professional development, resources, staffing qualifications, meals, and more. The study concluded that early childhood leaders should be knowledgeable about "early childhood development and best practices if they are to support and lay the groundwork for early childhood education" (p. 263).

What's often overlooked is the ripple effect of professional contentment on retention rates. A teacher who views their role not as a dead-end job but as a vibrant path with growth opportunities is far more likely to stay and contribute meaningfully. This chapter unpacks the intrinsic link between comprehensive professional development programs and heightened teacher retention. Drawing from real-world scenarios, studies, and expert testimonies, the impact of these initiatives is examined through a clear and detailed lens.

Identifying the impact requires us to scrutinize teacher satisfaction metrics and their correlation with professional growth prospects. It is well-documented through educational research that career advancement opportunities are among the top factors influencing an educator's decision to remain in their position. A narrative emerges from the data: when teachers are supported in their professional journey, they feel valued and are more inclined to invest their skills and loyalty in the institution that supports them.

However, to comprehend the full narrative, it's crucial to learn actionable strategies. These strategies are not just concepts but tested methods that align with the goal of nurturing talent within the tight constraints of the educational sector. The chapter presents a toolkit filled with innovation and practicality designed to help early childhood directors create and maintain opportunities for teacher development, even amidst resource challenges.

As you embark on the exploration of these growth opportunities, you will find that they are not just interventions but are a testament to the belief in the transformational power of learning—not only for children but for the educators guiding them. Continuous professional development is the bedrock of a resilient educational workforce, fostering not just improved teaching practices but also personal fulfillment and a sense of community among educators.

Together, by valuing diverse perspectives, we can construct a culture that whole-heartedly embraces growth, ensuring that no teacher's potential is left untapped. This is a charge not just for the individual but for the collective, driving forward the narrative that professional development is not just an option but an imperative—for the teachers, the students, and the future of education itself.

Through thoughtful examination and strategic action, this chapter lays out the roadmap to a reality where professional stagnation is a thing of the past, and every teacher has the means to excel within the educational landscape—thus securing the strength and vibrancy of our early childhood education system.

Investing in ongoing professional development and career advancement opportunities for teacher retention is essential in creating a thriving and successful educational environment. Teachers who feel supported, valued, and provided with growth opportunities are more likely to stay in their positions, contributing to higher teacher retention rates. When educators receive ongoing training, they are equipped with the skills and knowledge needed to excel in the classroom, leading to increased self-actualization and self-efficacy, a direct correlation to job satisfaction and effectiveness.

Professional growth opportunities not only benefit individual teachers but also have positive effects on the overall quality of education. Teachers who have access to career advancement opportunities are more likely to feel motivated and fulfilled in their roles, which directly impacts the learning experience of their students. By investing in the professional development of teaching staff, early childhood programs can cultivate a culture of continuous improvement and innovation, ensuring that the children in their care receive the best possible education.

Moreover, prioritizing professional development and career advancement opportunities communicates a strong message of commitment and support to the teaching staff. When educators feel that their professional growth is valued and supported, they are more likely to develop a strong sense of loyalty and dedication to the organization. This level of support fosters a positive work environment where teachers feel empowered to contribute their best efforts, knowing that their growth is a priority for the program.

Research supports the importance of ongoing professional development and career advancement opportunities in teacher retention. Additionally, the early childhood education standards, curriculum, and increased emphasis on accountability are all changing quickly. Haslip and Gullo (2017) looked at how these changes are affecting professional development. They examined "the landscape of early childhood education is rapidly changing... driven by positive and negative trends" (p. 250). Financial support is lacking in the early childhood sector to sustain the rapidly changing early childhood landscape in areas such as in-service and pre-service teacher preparation, professional development, resources, staffing qualifications, meals, and more. The study concluded that early childhood leaders should be knowledgeable about "early childhood development and best practices if they are to support and lay the groundwork for early childhood education" (p. 263).

As you continue reading, you'll discover the undeniable impact of prioritizing professional growth on teacher satisfaction and retention and gain insights into actionable strategies for providing meaningful growth opportunities for teaching staff.

Prioritizing professional growth and development opportunities has a profound impact on teacher satisfaction and retention. **When teachers are given access to ongoing training, career advancement opportunities, and professional development, they have a feeling of self-actualization; they feel valued and recognized for their contributions.** This sense of acknowledgment and investment in their growth leads to heightened job satisfaction, ultimately translating into higher retention rates within the early childhood program. Studies have consistently shown that organizations that prioritize the growth and development of their employees experience lower turnover and higher levels of employee satisfaction. By extending this principle to the context of early childhood programs, it's clear that investing in the professional growth of teachers can significantly impact their willingness to stay in their roles.

When teachers perceive that their professional growth is prioritized, they are more likely to feel a sense of purpose and fulfillment in their roles. **The opportunity for continuous learning and development empowers them to elevate their skills and stay engaged in their work**. This can also have a positive ripple effect on the overall quality of education provided to the children. Teachers who feel supported in their professional growth are more likely to bring enthusiasm and commitment to their classrooms, which greatly benefits the young students under their care.

Moreover, providing teachers with access to career advancement opportunities can instill a strong sense of loyalty and commitment. **When educators see a clear path for growth and advancement within their organization, they are more inclined to stay and invest in their long-term success.** This not only promotes a stable and dedicated teaching staff but also fosters a culture of growth and progression within the program. The anticipation of possible promotions or advancements can serve as a powerful motivator for teachers, driving them to continuously improve their skills and contribute to the overall success of the program.

In addition to satisfaction and commitment, prioritizing professional growth can also have a direct impact on the retention of high-performing teachers. **When these educators are offered opportunities for personal and professional improvement, they are more likely to stay in their roles, knowing that their contributions are valued and their growth is supported**. This helps to build a team of skilled and experienced teachers, which is integral for maintaining the high-quality educational experience that early childhood and Head Start programs strive to provide for children. Retaining top talent is key to creating a stable and supportive learning environment for both teachers and students.

In the next section, we will delve into actionable strategies for providing meaningful growth opportunities for teaching staff. It is crucial to recognize the specific avenues through which professional development and career advancement can be effectively integrated into the fabric of a program. By understanding these strategies, program directors can navigate a deliberate path toward sustaining high teacher retention and fostering an environment of continuous growth and improvement for all stakeholders involved.

Creating a culture of growth within begins with recognizing that **professional development** is not just an administrative checkbox but a pathway to personal fulfillment and organizational success. Early childhood directors can implement a variety of actionable strategies designed to provide meaningful growth opportunities that resonate deeply with teaching staff. The goal here is to foster an environment of **lifelong learning**, directly influencing teacher satisfaction and corresponding retention rates.

ACTIONABLE STRATEGIES FOR GROWTH

PERSONALIZED PROFESSIONAL DEVELOPMENT PLANS

As discussed in the previous chapter, one robust strategy is the creation of personalized professional development plans. Tailoring learning and development to the individual needs and goals of each teacher demonstrates respect for their unique career aspirations. Hold regular meetings with teaching staff to establish short-term and long-term career objectives. Establishing these goals illuminates a path for educators to advance their expertise while signaling that their professional aspirations are supported and valued.

MENTORSHIP PROGRAMS

A mentorship program can be an invaluable asset, linking less experienced teachers with seasoned veterans. These relationships can enhance teaching skills, offer emotional support, and provide guidance through the complexity of early childhood education. More than just a transfer of knowledge, mentorship helps build a supportive community within the program and catalyzes the professional growth of both mentors and mentees.

CROSS-TRAINING OPPORTUNITIES

Implementing cross-training opportunities encourages teachers to learn about roles and responsibilities outside their usual remits. This approach not only builds flexibility and resilience within your team but also broadens the professional skill sets of individual staff members. Cross-training can reveal latent talents and foster a deeper understanding of the program as a holistic entity, enabling teachers to appreciate their role in the larger mission of early childhood education.

INVESTING IN EDUCATOR CERTIFICATIONS

Investing in certifications or advanced degrees for your teaching staff is a significant but impactful strategy. Financial assistance or flexible scheduling to support continuing education can be a clear sign of commitment to staff growth. It also ensures that your program benefits from the most current and advanced educational practices, raising the standard of teaching and learning within your organization.

FOSTERING LEADERSHIP SKILLS

Identifying potential leaders among your teaching staff and fostering their abilities can be transformational for them and the program. Initiating leadership development programs or offering roles with increased responsibilities paves the way for career advancement. This proactive approach to career development can motivate teachers, providing a clear route to leadership positions within the organization.

CONTINUOUS FEEDBACK AND RECOGNITION

A culture of continuous feedback can greatly enhance the growth opportunities for staff. Constructive feedback helps teachers to refine their practice, while recognition of achievements fosters a sense of accomplishment and belonging. Celebrate teacher successes through awards, acknowledgments in meetings, or profiles in newsletters. Public recognition not only boosts individual morale but also underscores the value placed on professional excellence within your program.

COLLABORATION WITH ACADEMIC INSTITUTIONS

Partnering with local colleges and universities to allow teachers to engage with cutting-edge practices and research in early childhood education can be especially enriching. This can take the form of guest lectures, workshops, or even collaborative research projects. Such partnerships can engender a sense of intellectual vitality among staff and position your program as a leader in the field.

In summary, the strategies delineated here revolve around creating a framework where teachers feel valued, supported, and equipped to navigate their professional journeys. The investment in professional development is an investment in teacher retention, cultivating an environment where teachers can both grow personally and contribute meaningfully to the visionary mission.

Investing in ongoing professional development and career advancement opportunities for teaching staff is pivotal to improving teacher retention. This chapter has delved into the significance of prioritizing professional growth and the impact it has on teacher satisfaction and retention. We've explored actionable strategies for providing meaningful growth opportunities for teaching staff, highlighting the transformational power of learning and development.

By acknowledging the importance of continual growth for educators and creating a supportive environment that fosters their advancement, early childhood directors can significantly improve teacher retention rates. **The commitment to the growth and success of teaching staff not only enhances job satisfaction but also signals a profound dedication to their long-term professional development.** When teachers feel valued and supported, they are more likely to remain in their roles, which ultimately benefits the entire early childhood education community.

It is imperative for early childhood leaders to **embrace a culture of learning and growth within their organization**, offering not only traditional training but also career advancement opportunities, mentorship programs, and access to relevant resources. By doing so, they can pave the way for a more stable and motivated teaching staff, resulting in a more effective and thriving early childhood education environment.

As we move forward, let's continue to explore and implement innovative approaches that prioritize professional development and growth opportunities, ultimately **creating an environment where teaching staff can flourish and contribute meaningfully to the lives of the children they serve.**

CHAPTER 8

LEADERSHIP FRAMEWORK

BACKGROUND

In the softly lit infants' room, Emma, the childcare center director, stood on the edge of a small Kermit-green mat where tiny bodies were napping. Her gaze was lost in thought; the rhythmic rise and fall of her chest synchronized with the gentle, slumberous breaths of the children. It was mid-morning, a time when the sun spilled its light like golden maple over the room, but there was a chill in the room that no amount of Southern California sunshine could dispel. What warmth there was came from the children, little embers of potentiality.

She prided herself on resilience and her ability to be the transformational leader her staff needed. Every issue seemed to be a puzzle she could piece together, but lately, the pieces felt like they were from different boxes. Emma understood too well that her teachers, nurturing as they were, grappled with the same existential needs detailed by Maslow, seeking purpose and fulfillment beyond their immediate responsibilities.

As Emma observed her teachers interact with the children – lifting, feeding, comforting – her thoughts wandered to a study she had read, which underlined an alarming trend: despite providing a head start for many students, a significant number of teachers were not 'finishing the race.' It drew her to reflect on the emotional and professional support her staff required, drawing parallels with Maslow's hierarchy. "Even though they care for the foundational needs of these children, who is caring for theirs?" she mused.

A soft laugh from one of the toddlers interrupted her train of thought, the small, chubby hands reaching out for his teacher, seeking assurance. This interaction was a snapshot, a tender reminder of the dependency on human connection, trust, and nurturing – the soft soil in which the roots of transformational leadership may firmly embed.

As Emma contemplated how her leadership practices could better address the teachers' needs, her mind wove through the intricacies of aligning emotional support with professional development. The teaching staff were more than caregivers; they were pillars upon which the children's entire early educational framework rested. "If the roots are not watered, how can the tree stand tall and give shade?" she thought, her mind relating the survival of the majestic oaks outside to the sustenance of her devoted staff.

Her day carried on – meetings, planning, moments of quiet mentoring – but the questions entrenched in transformational leadership and the hierarchy of needs spiraled within her. The soft hum of the air conditioner, the distant sound of playful shrieks from outside, and the occasional coo from an infant all merged into the background.

Emma knew that this was more than a mere operational exercise. This was about creating a sanctuary for her teachers that was as comforting and supportive as the environment they provided for the children. As the clock neared noon and the sounds of laughter signaled the end of nap time, Emma's determination solidified, "These teachers nurture growth, but am I nurturing theirs effectively?"

As Edwards Deming once said, "A bad system will beat a good person every time." Was the current system overlooking the teachers' professional fulfillment? How could transformational leadership foster an inclusive sanctuary, not just for the children but also for those crafting the future one gentle interaction at a time?

TRANSFORMATIONAL LEADERSHIP

With educational settings continually evolving, the challenge to retain qualified and committed teaching staff has become more pronounced than ever. Leaders within these environments are tasked with adopting innovative strategies to ensure that stability is not just an outcome but a prominent feature of their organizational culture. A transformational leadership approach provides the guidance needed in the behaviors of the teachers and the leaders. It provides a "cause and effect" analysis by determining why teachers leave and what leaders can do to help prevent this.

John Maxwell (2022) asserted that "everything rises and falls on leadership… but knowing how to lead is only half the battle" (p. 1). The definitions of leadership have evolved since the 1900s, including ideas such as emphasizing "control and the centralization of power" including leadership styles such as transformational leadership (Northouse, 2019, p. 2). If leadership theories are not understood and applied improperly, leadership power can cause toxicity and be harmful to a group, or it can be a tool to positively change an organization (Northouse, 2019). Additionally, it can be challenging for leadership to remove obstacles, such as supporting and meeting the needs of teachers, hiring qualified staff, eliminating excessive workloads and burnout, and providing staff development while motivating and inspiring teachers to achieve high student outcomes when they are not well-prepared to lead an organization (Barnett, 2002; Brill & McCartney, 2008; Darling-Hammond et al., 2005; Hart & Schumacher, 2005).

Up until the 1970s, most leadership theories were based on traits, task-oriented skills, and characteristics. However, James MacGregor Burns, a political sociologist, produced a new paradigm shift known as transformational leadership, which he defined as "a process that changes and transforms people" (Northouse, 2019, p. 163). According to Bass (1985), transformational leadership has four primary characteristics: charisma, inspirational leadership, individualized consideration, and intellectual stimulation (see Figure 1). Transformational leaders consider the motivations of their followers, meet their needs, and treat them as complete individuals. Leaders utilizing this new theory lead followers through change and transformation within their organizations with a "growing self-awareness" (Bryman, 1999, p. 32) of vision and mission in mind and without controlling individuals.

Figure 1. Transformational Leadership

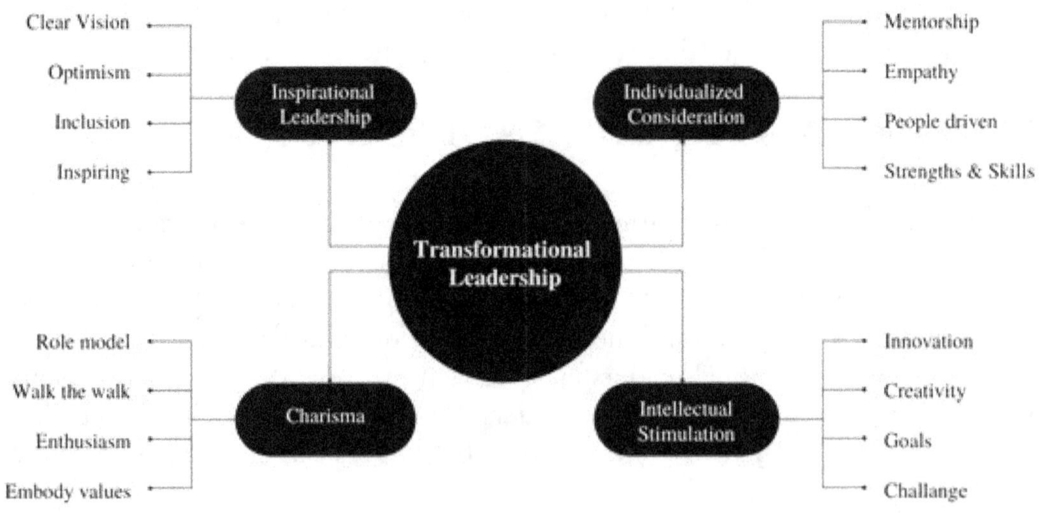

Note: The Transformational Leadership figure above has been adapted from SimplyPsychology by C. Ugochukwu, 2023, www.simplypsychology. copyright (2023).

Transformational leadership is essential in the school setting since this leadership style is constantly looking for methods to create a positive organizational culture. Transformational leaders "build trust and foster collaboration with others" and are "out front advocating change" (Northouse, 2019, pp. 178-179). Grantham-Caston and DiCarlo (2021) found that transformational leaders instill trust in their team members and foster an environment that supports their professional development. Transformational leaders provide individual support and personal attention to each teacher to allow them to reach their goals (Northouse, 2019). They provide classroom observations, give immediate feedback, and encourage goal setting to increase teaching techniques and student outcomes. In a study conducted by Brill and McCartney (2008), large class sizes, heavy workloads, and poor mentoring were examples of leadership inadequacy. Applying the transformational leadership concept in the early childhood setting allows the administrator to focus on implementing a positive cultural change by creating an environment where teachers are provided pedagogical guidance, supported with challenging behaviors, and praised for their accomplishments and efforts.

Leadership isn't atop a formal hierarchy but at the heart of the organization. Here, we unpack the principles of transformational leadership—inspiring but also providing a clear vision and solidarity. Directors are not just managers. They're conductors guiding a symphony of learning.

Let me tell you about a Head Start program that underwent a metamorphosis, all thanks to the power of transformational leadership! Picture this: Lakeside Head Start (fictional name), nestled in the heart of a bustling community, but it was a diamond in the rough, rough that only visionary eyes could see through. In came center director Michael, a beacon of change whose infectious energy was impossible to ignore.

I watched in awe as center director Michael took the reins, not from an ivory tower, but right there, on the ground, side-by-side with the teachers. They transformed halls that echoed with uncertainty into halls reverberating with the sizzling energy of possibility. Friday afternoons used to signal the end of a draining week, but under Michaels's leadership, they became 'Future Fridays,' a time for teachers to gather, share victories, and set goals with cheers and refreshments in hand.

Lakeside's transformation was tangible. Teachers once weary of monotonous training sessions now engaged in dynamic professional development workshops tailored to their needs—because that's what transformational leaders do: they amplify voices, fuel dreams, and craft runways for take-offs into excellence. Students, who were mere consumers of knowledge, became little champions steering their own learning ships.

One year later—a splash of color here, an empowered teacher there, classrooms humming with engaged learners everywhere—Lakeside became the talk of the town. Children became kinder-ready, parents became engaged, and the community became invested. That, my friends, is the undeniable mark of transformational leadership. It wasn't just a change but a revolution, a narrative weaved with the golden threads of inspiration, support, and unabashed enthusiasm. This is the model every educational leader should aspire to, a beacon that shines a light on potential and primes that potential to blossom to its fullest. Are you ready to be the transformational leader your Head Start or early childhood program so richly deserves? Join us, and let's raise the bar together higher than ever before!

Leadership that is transformational by nature is not only reactive but also proactive. It seeks to restructure the teaching environment to be one that is inclusive, nurturing, and supportive of growth. This is where the classic Maslow's Hierarchy of Needs intersects with modern leadership strategies. By applying this psychological framework, childcare directors can effectively identify and prioritize the intrinsic motivations and needs that drive teacher satisfaction and commitment.

For early childhood professionals who invest their energies in cultivating young minds, work is more than just a paycheck; it involves a search for purpose and the fulfillment that comes from making a significant impact. Aligning leadership practices with these deep-seated needs fosters an environment where teachers feel understood, valued, and motivated. This alignment is crucial because it directly influences teacher retention, which is the bedrock of a stable and thriving educational institution.

Nurturing begins with communication. Creating channels for open discussion and feedback sets the stage for a collaborative atmosphere. It's about building a community of professionals where each is heard, recognized, and given the platform to grow. Through structured mentorship and collective planning, leaders can galvanize the spirit of togetherness and intellectual sharing while ensuring that everyone moves in tandem towards shared objectives.

Professional development is a cornerstone. By championing continuous learning and providing resources for teachers to augment their skills, directors emphasize the importance of progression in careers. Whether it involves sponsoring further education or creating opportunities for pioneer thinking at educational conferences, it is about sending a clear message: the growth of the teachers is pivotal for the growth of the institution.

Recognizing the human element in education is critical. Teachers, like all individuals, crave acknowledgment and appreciation. Addressing this through both formal recognition systems and the integration of teachers in decision-making processes bolsters a sense of ownership and pride in their work. These initiatives can transform the workplace into a nurturing habitat where educators flourish.

THE BLUEPRINT OF SUPPORTIVE HARMONICS.

To embark on this transformational journey, consider the following step-by-step process—The Blueprint of Supportive Harmonics—with a clear end goal: embedding stability into the fabric of your teaching community.

STEP 1: CULTIVATE OPEN DISCOURSE

BEGIN BY ENCOURAGING A CULTURE WHERE COMMUNICATION THRIVES.

- Dedicate time for regular team meetings to share experiences, challenges, and triumphs.
- Design avenues for teachers to voice their ideas and concerns, respecting anonymity when Preferred.
- Pair seasoned educators with newcomers to foster mentorship bonds.
- Encourage collective curriculum crafting to integrate diverse perspectives and expertise.

Timeframe: Gradually integrate these practices over a period of 1-2 months, allowing staff to acclimatize to the improved communication flow.

STEP 2: PROPEL PROFESSIONAL EXPANSION

Provide pathways for professional growth.

• Offer workshops and access to recent educational research to keep teaching methods fresh and effective.
• Support aspirations for advanced qualifications through learning incentives.
• Facilitate participation in educational symposiums to build a repertoire of professional contacts.

Timeframe: Set annual professional development goals to measure progress and adapt strategies accordingly.

STEP 3: APPLAUD AND REWARD

Acknowledge efforts and milestones.

• Commemorate teachers' achievements and team milestones regularly.
• Establish incentive programs that add tangible value to outstanding contributions.
• Provide constructive and balanced feedback aiming to elevate teaching practices.

Timeframe: Each term, integrate new recognition practices to maintain momentum and inject novelty into appreciation methods.

STEP 4: BALANCE LIFE'S SYMPHONY

Promote equilibrium between work and personal life.

• Respect work boundaries and encourage the use of leave for rejuvenation.
  o Refrain from calling hourly staff to work on tasks outside of the work schedule.
• Offer support for stress management through wellness programs.
• Be flexible with schedules, especially for those juggling family and work.

Timeframe: Seek feedback every 6 months to adjust offerings that best support work-life balance

STEP 5: SHAPE THE ENVIRONMENT

Ensure a physical space that inspires teaching and learning.

• Regularly update and maintain decor and materials to support a stimulating classroom experience.
• Refrain from colors that will overly stimulate the children.
• Provide areas for staff relaxation to enhance comfort and well-being.
• Continuously improve the overall ambiance and aesthetics to positively influence mood and productivity.

Timeframe: Biannually, review the physical environment and plan improvements as necessary.

By diligently following these steps, the outcome is a more harmonious, productive, and sustainable work environment—a sanctuary where teachers feel empowered to thrive both professionally and personally. Success manifests in the increased retention of contented and motivated educators, a robust indication of the health of your educational establishment.

Transformative leadership in early childhood education centers is essential for creating an inclusive and nurturing environment for teachers. By adopting a transformational leadership approach, childcare directors can empower their staff, promote collaboration, and develop a sense of purpose and fulfillment. Through this leadership style, directors can foster an environment where teachers feel valued, respected, and supported, ultimately leading to increased teacher retention and program quality.

One of the core principles of transformational leadership is the emphasis on building strong relationships and trust among team members. This means actively listening to their staff, understanding their needs, and providing the necessary support. It involves creating a culture of open communication, constructive feedback, and mutual respect. By investing in building positive relationships with their teachers, directors can create a foundation for a collaborative and supportive work environment.

Moreover, transformational leadership encourages continuous growth and learning. Directors can facilitate professional development opportunities for their teachers, provide access to training, and create a culture of learning within the organization. This could include workshops, seminars, or access to resources to aid in their skill development.

Recognizing the strengths and potential of each teacher is another aspect of transformational leadership. By acknowledging the unique contributions and strengths of their staff, directors can foster a sense of belonging and significance. This form of positive reinforcement can significantly impact the motivation and morale of the teaching staff.

Furthermore, transformational leadership involves setting a clear vision and direction for the organization. By communicating a compelling and inspiring vision, directors can align the efforts of the teaching staff with the broader goals of the center. When educators understand the purpose and direction of their work, they are more likely to feel motivated and dedicated to their roles.

Implementing a transformational leadership approach is not only beneficial for the teaching staff but also for the overall success of the program. By fostering an inclusive and nurturing environment, directors can significantly contribute to teacher retention and program quality, making a positive impact on the lives of children and families.

THE HUMAN MOTIVATION THEORY

Unlocking the secrets to a truly nurturing work environment goes beyond transformational leadership. We will now dive into the powerful insights of Human Motivation Theory and its role in building a supportive and nurturing work environment that keeps your valuable staff members happy and engaged.

Understanding Maslow's Hierarchy of Needs is crucial for childcare directors seeking to create a supportive and stable work environment for their teaching staff. Abraham Maslow's theory posits that individuals are motivated by a hierarchy of needs, with basic physiological needs at the bottom and self-actualization at the top. For early childhood professionals, this theory provides valuable insights into the fundamental needs that drive their behavior and job satisfaction.

Human needs exist within a complex hierarchy, with each level needing something more than the one before it. This concept was created by psychologist Abraham H. Maslow (1943). He noticed that people would always start at their most basic requirements for survival, such as food and shelter. He believed this is how people should think about societal levels rather than just focusing on materialistic things like money or status symbols, which can often come alongside healthy relationships with others. Therefore, the theory of human motivation was a significant piece of the conceptual framework for the study. "Even though Students Are Getting A Head Start, Why Aren't Teachers Finishing The Race?'"

According to the theory (Maslow, 1943), the five levels of human behavior are physiological needs, safety concerns (i.e., feeling safe), social factors, which include having friends around you when going about daily activities, etc.; self-esteem refers to self-respect/self-worth issues regarding oneself, and self-actualization, the longing to become better. People are driven by the desire to attain or preserve the many conditions underpinning fundamental fulfillments and goals that are more introspective. According to Maslow, when one need is sufficiently met, a subsequent need arises, and the failure to supply any of these needs results in a physiological risk.

In order to retain early childhood educators in the profession, it is imperative that leadership meets the basic needs of individuals in the workplace. As seen in Figure 2, the first basic need is physiological needs.

At the foundational level of Maslow's Hierarchy of Needs are **physiological needs** such as food, water, and rest. Without meeting these basic needs, teachers may struggle to focus on their work, leading to decreased job satisfaction and performance. The **physiological need** for early childhood educators is to be equitably compensated for one's work and provided with basic medical coverage. Without this, people cannot provide food and shelter on their behalf and offer financial or medical support.

Moving up the hierarchy, safety needs are paramount for early childhood professionals. Job security, a safe and clean working environment, and clear policies for handling emergencies are essential for teachers to feel secure in their roles. When childcare directors take action to ensure the safety and security of their staff, it fosters a sense of trust and stability, laying the foundation for a positive work environment. A poor work environment and lack of support for challenging behaviors are factors contributing to the sense of job dissatisfaction.

Another basic need is **social support** (Maslow, 1943). Social factors, such as having a positive relationship with the leader, are essential in determining why some teachers leave their jobs. The lack of administrative assistance or acknowledgment is one primary reason that leads teachers towards quitting school or changing careers, which often results in no resolution and contributes to more stress.

The fourth basic need is **self-esteem** (Maslow, 1943). **Self-esteem needs** revolve around the desire for recognition, respect, and a sense of accomplishment. Teachers want to feel heard and respected. They need a voice in and out of the classroom that they can rely on, so it is essential for them to not only be knowledgeable but also to express their feelings, when necessary, about challenging topics or student outcomes. Teachers not being heard leads to an internal shutdown and an intention to quit. Teachers also want to feel valued and respected. Illegitimate tasks, "tasks that violate norms about what an employee can reasonably be expected to do," result in teachers feeling humiliated or undignified (Eatough et al., 2015, p. 108).

When childcare directors acknowledge the hard work and dedication of their staff, it boosts their morale and sense of self-worth. Providing opportunities for professional development, recognizing achievements, and fostering a culture of appreciation are vital steps toward fulfilling the esteem needs of early childhood professionals

At the pinnacle of Maslow's Hierarchy of Needs is **self-actualization**, representing the desire for personal growth and fulfillment. The need for professional development is a significant source of frustration for teachers. When they lack this necessary development, it limits educators' growth potential. It keeps them from reaching self-actualization - an ideal state where one's talents are used to the fullest extent possible (Maslow, 1943).

Childcare directors can facilitate self-actualization among their staff by encouraging autonomy, creativity, and innovation in teaching methods. By providing opportunities for professional growth, nurturing individual talents, and empowering teachers to reach their full potential, directors can cultivate a work environment where self-actualization is not just a goal but a reality for their teaching staff.

TEACHER HIERARCHY OF NEEDS

Figure 2. Maslow's Hierarchy of Needs Adapted to Teacher Needs

Note: Maslow's Hierarchy of Needs Adapted to Teacher Needs above has been adapted from CSA education by L. Panka, 2022 www.csaedu.com. Copyright (2023).

Let me tell you a story—one that will light a fire in your heart and show you the power of transformation. There was a center director, we'll call her Ms. Amerie, whose passion for education was as vast as the ocean. When Ms. Amerie stepped into her role, the center she inherited was struggling; teachers felt undervalued, the atmosphere was disheartening, and creativity was as scarce as rain in a desert.

But Ms. Amerie saw not a barren land but a fertile ground for growth. With a heart full of enthusiasm and a plethora of experience, she embarked on a journey to revitalize her center by meeting Maslow's Hierarchy of Needs head-on.

She started at the base—safety. Keep in mind that compensation should be the base; however, the center director did not have control of pay. So, she began with safety. Ms. Amerie reimagined the center as a sanctuary where teachers felt secure and supported. "Your voice is not just heard here; it echoes," she'd proclaim. She introduced structures that ensured teachers had the tools and resources they needed, breeding a culture where stress dwindled and spirits soared.

Next up, relationships. Ms. Amerie was positive that a happy center was one where everyone felt connected. She fostered trust and camaraderie through team-building activities. "We're in this together," she'd remind her team as they shared stories and laughs. The walls of isolation crumbled, replaced by bridges of kinship.

When it came to esteem, Ms. Amerie was determined to make each educator feel like a super-hero. Recognition became her secret weapon, from celebrating 'Teacher of the Month' to simple 'glows and grows' notes. "Your work is heroic," she'd say, eyes sparkling with sincerity, "and heroes deserve to be celebrated!"

Finally, self-actualization—Ms. Amerie's favorite chapter. She nurtured an environment where teachers were encouraged to dream big and pursue personal goals. Professional development wasn't just available; it was customized. She implemented individual professional development plans. "Grow into your greatness," she'd cheer, inspiring her staff to reach heights they never thought possible.

The transformation was miraculous. Ms. Amerie's center blossomed, a place where fulfillment was the norm, and every day brimmed with the possibility of greatness. Her passionate leadership had done more than change a center; it had ignited a beacon of hope, proving that with the right support, every educator has the potential to flourish.

In conclusion, Maslow's Hierarchy of Needs offers a valuable framework for understanding the fundamental motivators that drive teacher behavior and job satisfaction. By recognizing and addressing these needs, childcare directors can foster a supportive and nurturing environment that empowers their staff to thrive both personally and professionally.

ALIGN FRAMEWORK

When stepping into the world of early childhood education as a leader, one of the pivotal tasks is to align one's leadership practices with the emotional and professional needs of the teaching staff. This harmonization is not just beneficial but essential for teacher retention. To aid in this effort, we introduce the ALIGN Framework - a methodical tool designed to evaluate and strengthen various teacher retention strategies.

ASSESSING TEACHER NEEDS

The first step in the ALIGN framework requires an honest assessment of the individual and collective needs of the teaching staff. This analysis should be rooted in Maslow's Hierarchy of Needs, taking into account personal growth, job security, a sense of belonging, and recognition. By understanding these needs, a director can tailor strategies that are both supportive and empowering.

LEVERAGING RESOURCES

Once the needs are established, it's crucial to leverage the available resources to meet them effectively. This could involve reallocating funds to provide competitive salaries, offering comprehensive benefits, and ensuring a safe and well-equipped work environment. Resources should also extend to professional development opportunities, creating pathways for teachers to enhance their skills and progress in their careers.

IMPACT ANALYSIS

Any strategy implemented requires an impact analysis to determine its effectiveness. For the ALIGN framework, the impact is measured by improvements in job satisfaction, teacher engagement, and, ultimately, retention rates. Keeping a pulse on these benchmarks helps to fine-tune strategies and create a responsive leadership approach that adapts to the evolving needs of staff.

GOAL ALIGNMENT

For strategies to be successful, they must align with the overarching goals of the early childhood center. These goals typically pertain to the quality of education, the well-being of the children, and the center's reputation in the community. ALIGN ensures that retention strategies support these end goals without compromising on the quality of care and education provided.

NURTURING RELATIONSHIPS

Central to the ALIGN framework is the nurturing of positive relationships among staff members and between staff and leadership. This component underscores the importance of a collaborative and respectful work culture. Through team-building activities, open communication, and a shared vision, the framework promotes cohesiveness within the educational community.

GROWTH AND DEVELOPMENT

Continuous growth and development are paramount in retaining early childhood educators. The framework stipulates offering supportive pathways for career advancement, including mentoring, coaching, and access to educational resources. This shows commitment to the teachers' professional journeys, which, in turn, fosters loyalty and a long-term commitment to the center.

As childcare centers implement the ALIGN framework, they set forth to ensure strategies are not standalone efforts but interconnected threads that together strengthen the fabric of an institution. By measuring and responding to the effectiveness of various teacher retention initiatives, directors can cultivate an environment where every educator not only feels valued and understood but is also given the tools and opportunities to grow and succeed.

Through ALIGN, directors can confidently address both the emotional and professional spheres of their staff's needs, thereby unlocking the full potential of their teams and creating a refuge of stability for the children they serve. This alignment is not a one-time act but a constant pursuit, one that evolves with time and necessitates unwavering dedication and insight. It is a pathway toward transforming an early childhood center into a beacon of innovation, compassion, and unmatched teaching excellence.

In this chapter, we have delved into the significance of transformational leadership and Maslow's Hierarchy of Needs in the context of early childhood education. The understanding that transformational **leadership** can create an inclusive and nurturing environment for early childhood professionals seeking purpose and fulfillment in their work is pivotal. Likewise, the application of **Maslow's Hierarchy of Needs** can help childcare directors recognize and address the fundamental needs that drive teacher behavior, ultimately fostering a stable and supportive work environment.

Drawing upon research by scholars such as Northouse (2019) and Maslow (1943), it is evident that a transformational leadership approach aligns with the emotional and professional needs of the teaching staff. As we have learned from **Maslow's Hierarchy of Needs**, addressing the fundamental needs of safety, belonging, and esteem can pave the way for professional growth and fulfillment in the workplace.

By integrating these frameworks into the leadership practices of childcare directors, we can expect to witness a positive shift in the work environment, with increased retention, job satisfaction, and overall well-being among early childhood professionals. It is essential for childcare directors to recognize the potential for transformational change by embracing transformational **leadership** and the principles of **Maslow's Hierarchy of Needs.** These frameworks not only contribute to the well-being of the teaching staff but also create an environment that nurtures the development of young children.

CHAPTER 9

THE ROLE OF EFFECTIVE LEADERSHIP IN TEACHER RETENTION

BACKGROUND

In the newborn silence of the early afternoon, Melissa found herself wandering through the halls of her childcare program, the echoes of children's laughter still whispering their secrets to the brightly painted walls. Outside, the sun toyed with the leaves of the old oak tree, casting a dance of shadows across the playground, now emptied of its little occupants.

Her office felt different with the door closed behind her—a sanctuary within a sanctuary. On the edge of her desk, a stack of resumes from hopeful educators seemed to leer at her, each page a voice vying for attention in the quiet of her thoughts. She understood that these papers represented more than potential hires; they were the embodiment of a philosophy she held dear: leadership in support of education is not a position but a promise to nourish the minds that will, in turn, educate the youth.

As Melissa sifted through the resumes, the crisp rustle of paper punctuated her introspection with a rhythmic cadence. Her mind grappled with the weight of responsibility, understanding that the retention of these teachers, these purveyors of knowledge, would pivot on her capacity to lead with vision and empathy. Their talent was evident, their passion palpable even in the dry black ink—but would it be enough to thrive under her wing?

The flicker of her computer screen caught her eye, and with a few clicks, she was drawn into the research outlining the stark link between effective leadership and teacher retention. The articles spoke of environments where teachers felt supported and understood, where career progression wasn't just a ladder but a horizon. She pondered how to translate this knowledge into the tangible fabric of her center—how to embody the leadership that inspires and retains the gift of dedication.

Fostering this type of environment would require more than just good intentions, she knew. It hinged on authentic engagement with the teachers, investing in their growth, listening to their concerns, and acting on their suggestions. It was about creating a partnership between the director and the educators, one rooted in mutual respect and shared goals. Through the screen's glow, Melissa imagined the faces of her staff, considered their aspirations, and in the quiet, the seed of a plan began to germinate.

She stood and wandered to the window, gaze drifting over the playground where the shadows had grown a bit longer, the oak tree ever watchful. Leadership wasn't a solo act; it was a chorus, and she was merely the conductor, her baton ready to guide her teachers through their harmonious crescendo. But could she weave the threads of leadership support into a quilt warm enough to keep her teachers from seeking shelter elsewhere?

THE LINCHPIN OF LONGEVITY: LEADERSHIP'S MARK ON TEACHER TENURE

As we delve into the critical role of effective leadership within the realm of early childhood education, it is imperative to recognize that the trajectory of teacher retention and program quality often hinges on the subtleties of support and empowerment. Leadership is far more than a title; it embodies the catalyst for a more vibrant, collaborative, and sustainable teaching workforce. Leaders in early childhood programs possess the unique capacity to architect an environment that does not merely retain talent but rather emboldens it, fostering a community that educators aspire to be a part of long-term.

Retention rates in education not only signal stability but also reflect the quality and satisfaction within the teaching experience. It is no secret that the turnover across educational institutions chips at the bedrock of quality education. However, leaders who appreciate the nuances of **motivation, growth, and well-being** can significantly reverse this trend. As we navigate the interplay between leadership practices and teacher retention, the evidence is clear: supportive leaders lay the groundwork for more effective teaching staff and a superior educational experience for children.

Understanding the transformational power of leadership begins by acknowledging that teachers thrive under leaders who understand pedagogy, display empathy, create avenues for professional development, and endorse a culture of respect. These factors directly impact the day-to-day resilience of educators. To retain top talent, an early childhood program must be led by individuals who not only grasp the educational landscape but also excel in the human dimension of leadership. The ability of a leader to foster a **positive work environment** enhances the sense of belonging and purpose among staff, which is essential for sustained commitment to their role.

CULTIVATING A NURTURING ECOSYSTEM: BEYOND THE ADMINISTRATIVE VEIL

The pursuit of a nurturing professional environment is not achieved by happenstance. It requires leaders to be purposeful in constructing systems of support that address the multifaceted challenges faced by educators. Identifying the key factors in leadership support is not merely a theoretical exercise; it is a strategic one. Leaders must be adept at recognizing and implementing practical measures, such as mentorship programs, relevant professional development opportunities, and mechanisms for recognizing accomplishments, to keep the teaching staff engaged and invested in their roles.

Recognition of the impact of leadership on a work environment is two-fold. It encompasses understanding the intrinsic motivators of staff and acknowledging the extrinsic rewards that reinforce their commitment. By providing ongoing support, early childhood leaders act as the scaffolding upon which a teacher's career can be built and stabilized. The exemplary leader must bridge the gap between the needs of their staff and the limited resources often at hand. Here lies the true test of creative and adaptive leadership, one that has far-reaching implications for the resilience of educational practitioners.

A STRATEGIC BLUEPRINT: EMPOWERMENT THROUGH ITERATIVE LEADERSHIP

As the conversation turns to actionable strategies, leaders are reminded that the trajectory of empowerment is iterative. Each interaction, decision, and policy has the potential to incrementally shape the teaching environment for the better. Regular feedback loops, transparent communication channels, and an inclusive approach to decision-making can solidify trust and ensure that every teacher's voice is valued in the collaborative advancement of the program's mission.

To crystallize these concepts, evidence-based research illustrates a stark correlation between supportive leadership practices and diminished burnout rates among educators. Addressing factors such as autonomy, mastery, and purpose, leaders can markedly enhance job satisfaction and loyalty among their staff. **Effective leadership does not merely adjust to the existing environment; it anticipates future needs and prepares the workforce to meet them with confidence and vigor.**

The chapter ahead lays out a comprehensive framework to foster an ecosystem where **innovation, collaboration, and engagement** flourish. By employing real-world examples grounded in robust research, readers will be equipped with the hindsight necessary to lead proactively, rather than reactively, in the dynamic landscape of early childhood programs.

LEADERSHIP'S LEGACY: IMPACT BEYOND IMMEDIATE METRICS

Just as teachers mold future generations, leaders, in turn, shape the realities of their educators. Looking beyond the immediate metrics of retention, the qualitative imprint of effective leadership is felt in the enriched interactions between teachers and students, the dynamism of classroom environments, and the forward momentum of educational standards. Leaders must bear the mantle of responsibility with cognizance of its scope, for their influences resonate beyond the walls of their institutions into the communities they serve.

In the pursuit of a transformational impact within early childhood programs, each center director embodies not just an administrator but a herald of change. A leader's capacity to nurture their staff's talents and ambitions is not a side task; it is their central mission. The following insights will not only shed light on the theoretical underpinnings but also guide you on a practicable journey to elevate your leadership and, in turn, safeguard the future of your educators.

Effective leadership is fundamental to improving retention rates and enhancing the overall quality of education. When directors prioritize the well-being and professional development of their teachers, it can significantly impact teacher retention and create a positive work environment. By understanding the crucial role of effective leadership, early childhood programs can take proactive steps to support and retain teaching talent, ultimately benefiting the children in their care.

The research I conducted, "Even Though Students Are Getting A Head Start, Why Aren't Teachers Finishing the Race?" implies that strong leadership is directly linked to teacher retention in early childhood education. Directors who provide clear goals, meaningful feedback, and opportunities for professional growth are more likely to retain their teaching staff. Additionally, when leaders create a culture of support, empowerment, and open communication, teachers feel valued and are more likely to stay in their roles.

Moreover, effective leadership plays a **pivotal role in the quality of education** children receive. When teaching staff feel supported and encouraged by their leaders, they are better equipped to create engaging learning experiences for their students. This, in turn, leads to higher-quality education and better outcomes for the children.

Effective leadership is about **building a strong foundation** for teacher success. It involves providing mentoring and coaching, promoting a collaborative working environment, and ensuring that teachers have access to the resources they need to thrive. Furthermore, effective leadership encompasses the ability to foster a culture of continuous learning and growth, inspiring teachers to be their best and encouraging them to pursue ongoing professional development opportunities.

By understanding the profound impact of effective leadership in early childhood programs, leaders can be empowered to take proactive steps to enhance teacher retention and the overall quality of education. It is crucial for leaders to acknowledge the significant role they play in creating a supportive and thriving environment for their teaching staff, ultimately benefiting the children they serve.

Continue reading to discover the key factors in leadership support that contribute to retaining top teaching talent.

Effective leadership is a critical component of creating a nurturing and supportive environment for teaching staff in early childhood programs. When it comes to retaining top teaching talent, there are key factors in leadership support that play a significant role. Research has shown that strong, supportive leadership can directly impact teacher retention rates, job satisfaction, and the overall quality of education provided. By identifying and understanding these key factors, directors can empower themselves to become effective leaders who contribute to the positive work environment needed to retain top teaching talent.

KEY FACTORS OF LEADERSHIP SUPPORT

PROFESSIONAL DEVELOPMENT OPPORTUNITIES

Providing ample opportunities for professional growth and development is a key component of effective leadership support. Directors who prioritize ongoing training, workshops, and mentorship programs for their teaching staff demonstrate a commitment to their professional growth. According to my research, the need for professional development is a significant source of frustration for teachers. When they lack this necessary development, it limits educators' growth potential. It keeps them from reaching self-actualization - an ideal state where one's talents are used to the fullest extent possible (Maslow, 1943).

OPEN COMMUNICATION CHANNELS

Another crucial factor in leadership support is maintaining open communication channels with teaching staff. Leaders who are approachable and actively listen to the concerns and suggestions of their teachers create a culture of transparency and trust. This can be instrumental in boosting morale and job satisfaction. Research from my scholarly deliverable, "Even Though Students Are Getting A Head Start, Why Aren't Teachers Finishing The Race?", the lack of general communication was the fourth theme that both new and experienced Head Start center directors mentioned regarding the reasons why Head Start teachers are leaving the profession.

RECOGNITION AND APPRECIATION

Effective leaders understand the importance of recognizing and appreciating the hard work of their teaching staff. Expressing gratitude and acknowledging the contributions of teachers can go a long way in creating a positive work environment and fostering a sense of belonging. A report published by the Journal of Applied Psychology found that employees who feel valued and appreciated by their leaders are more likely to stay with the organization.

SUPPORT FOR WORK-LIFE BALANCE

Leaders who prioritize the well-being of their teaching staff by supporting a healthy work-life balance contribute to greater job satisfaction and retention rates. Directors can implement policies that support flexible work arrangements, allow for personal time off, and offer resources for managing stress and workload. My study also revealed the lack of acknowledgment is one primary reason that leads teachers towards quitting school or changing careers, which often results in no resolution and contributes to more stress.

CONFLICT RESOLUTION AND ADVOCACY

Successful leaders are adept at resolving conflicts and advocating for the needs of their teaching staff. When disputes or challenges arise, the ability of leaders to effectively address and resolve these issues can strengthen the mutual trust and respect between directors and teachers. Additionally, leaders who advocate for the needs of their teachers within the organization demonstrate a commitment to their well-being.

By understanding and implementing these key factors in leadership support, directors of early childhood programs can create an environment that nurtures and retains top teaching talent. These factors serve as foundational elements in building a positive work culture, fostering professional growth, and ultimately enhancing the quality of education provided to young children. When leaders prioritize the well-being and professional development of their teaching staff, they not only contribute to teacher retention but also create a supportive and thriving environment for both educators and students.

In conclusion, recognizing the significance of leadership support in retaining top teaching talent is paramount for the success of early childhood programs. By prioritizing professional development opportunities, open communication, recognition, support for work-life balance, and conflict resolution, effective leaders can make a tangible difference in improving teacher retention rates. This understanding empowers directors to take proactive steps in creating a supportive and thriving environment for their teaching staff.

CULTURE FRAMEWORK

ORGANIZATIONAL CULTURE

The bedrock of a thriving early childhood program is its organizational culture. An environment steeped in positive values and supportive interaction does not emerge by chance; it is the product of intentional leadership that understands the importance of a nurturing atmosphere. Leaders set the tone by exemplifying a sense of community, recognition, and respect that permeates through every tier of the organization. This cultural milieu serves as a safety net, empowering educators to take risks in their teaching and to grow from both their successes and their setbacks. When this strong foundation is in place, it acts as a magnet for teaching talent, inherently boosting retention through its affirming presence.

PROFESSIONAL DEVELOPMENT

Continual growth and learning are pivotal for teacher satisfaction and expertise. By prioritizing professional development, leaders in early childhood education demonstrate their commitment to their staff's personal and professional trajectories. Offering relevant training and skills enhancement opportunities not only equips teachers with the tools to succeed but also signals that their development is an organizational priority. It is essential for leaders to work with teaching staff to identify areas for growth and to provide resources tailored to individual and group needs. Done well, this component keeps teachers engaged, competent, and more likely to remain within a program that invests in their future.

MENTORSHIP AND COACHING

Mentorship and coaching extend beyond mere professional development. They build a bridge connecting the practical to the personal, offering guidance personalized to the teacher's needs and circumstances. A strong mentor or coaching program provides both newer and seasoned teachers with a sounding board for issues and a source of wisdom for pedagogical strategies. These relationships create a collegial atmosphere where teachers feel supported not just by the administration but also by their peers. The backing provided by mentors and coaches is crucial in encouraging teacher retention, as it directly influences a teacher's capability to manage classroom challenges and to nurture their own passion for the profession.

COLLABORATION AND COMMUNICATION

Among the strongest fibers that weave the fabric of a positive work environment are collaboration and communication. When teaching staff communicate openly and collaborate regularly, it fosters a sense of cohesion and shared purpose. Leaders must encourage an environment where team meetings, joint planning sessions, and peer feedback are the norm, as opposed to siloed, isolated work. This collegial approach leads to the cross-pollination of ideas, the sharing of best practices, and a supportive network that can help alleviate the stress and isolation that often come with teaching. Clear and consistent communication from leadership also plays a role in dispelling uncertainties and aligning the team toward common objectives.

WORK-LIFE BALANCE

Lastly, the rise of expectations and responsibilities in teaching has made work-life balance a critical aspect of job satisfaction. Leaders need to advocate for policies and practices that allow educators to manage their time and well-being effectively. This might be flexible work schedules, wellness programs, or simply an understanding culture that values personal time and boundaries. By acknowledging the importance of life outside of work, leaders impart a sense of respect for their staff's well-being, which, in turn, can foster greater loyalty and reduce burnout.

The components of the Culture Framework—Organizational Culture, Professional Development, Mentorship and Coaching, Collaboration and Communication, and Work-Life Balance—do not act in isolation. Instead, they form an interlocking system where the strength of one leverages the others, creating a stable and nurturing environment. This interconnectedness means that improvements in one area can positively affect the others, leading to a dynamic, self-reinforcing cycle that contributes to a robust and resilient program.

The practical implications are wide-ranging and deeply transformative. Its application elevates the work environment, enhances teacher efficacy, and, most fundamentally, improves retention rates. Over time, these benefits compound, leading to an institution recognized not simply for its commitment to early childhood education but also as a beacon for those educators who wish to grow, thrive, and make a long-lasting impact within their profession.

Effective leadership is the cornerstone of creating a supportive and thriving environment for teaching staff. By prioritizing the well-being and professional development of teachers, directors can significantly improve retention rates and enhance the overall quality of education in early childhood programs. When leaders actively support their teaching staff through mentorship, professional development opportunities, and a positive work culture, they foster a sense of value and satisfaction among teachers. This, in turn, **contributes to higher retention rates and a more conducive learning environment for young children**.

The key factors in leadership support, such as providing ongoing feedback, acknowledging the strengths of teachers, and promoting a collaborative work culture, play a pivotal role in retaining top teaching talent. Through these measures, leaders not only keep their best educators motivated and engaged, but they also attract new talent by creating a reputation for being an organization that values its teaching staff.

Furthermore, leadership support goes beyond retaining top talent and plays a crucial role in fostering a positive work environment. When teachers feel appreciated, supported, and part of a collaborative team, they are more likely to be satisfied with their jobs, experience less burnout, and deliver high-quality education to their students. **The positive impact of leadership support resonates throughout the entire program, influencing the well-being of the staff and the quality of education provided to children.**

By recognizing the importance of effective leadership and understanding its impact on teacher retention, we can empower early childhood directors to build a more fulfilling and supportive environment for their teaching staff. In the following chapters, we will delve deeper into strategies and actionable steps that directors can take to enhance their leadership skills and create a thriving, supportive culture within their programs.

CHAPTER 10

IMPLEMENTING EFFECTIVE LEADERSHIP SUPPORT

BACKGROUND

A gentle hum of voices murmured through the halls of Windermere ECE Center as the center director, Mr. Jacob, walked with an air of quiet determination. The sun was just beginning to dip below the tree line, casting a warm glow through the large windows of the school corridor. It was during these hours that the school seemed to exhale, releasing the tension of the day in a soft, warm sigh. Yet, for Mr. Jacob, the weight of leadership never truly lifted. It seemed ever-present, an invisible mantle that required not just the execution of duties but a deeper, more transformational impact.

The day's convocation remained fresh in his mind as he recounted the teachers' poignant tales of burnout. Mr. Jacob had always believed in the power of transformational leadership — the kind that could ignite passion and foster resilience. He felt the contours of the problem in his chest, the pressure to enact change, to be the beacon his teachers needed. They were on the precipice, and something had to shift. Inside his office, Mr. Jacob turned on an old brass lamp that cast shadows against the stacks of paperwork on his desk. But his thoughts weren't on reports or data; they were with his teachers, whose well-being was the bedrock of his students' success.

It was evident — that the center's environment needed nurturing. How could he ensure his leadership was effective enough to rekindle Mr. Lawrence's spirit and passion?

Eyes closed, he breathed deeply, searching for the insight that often visited his in stillness. His desk, a sea of responsibilities that stretched from corner to corner, no longer seemed daunting. Instead, it was a platform, a place from which he could orchestrate support and growth. Mr. Jacob knew that for his teachers to thrive and for student achievement to rise in kind, he had to cultivate an ethos of care, recognition, and genuine collaboration. He recalled the studies she had pored over, each underscoring the unequivocal link between strong leadership and teacher retention.

The pale light of the computer screen shimmered against his glasses as he organized an impromptu meeting for the following day. A leadership development seminar, perhaps, or a peer-mentoring program to foster connections that might buffer the stresses they faced. There was a solution woven within the problem, and he was determined to unravel it, thread by thread.

As he locked his office door and walked down the now quiet hall, a question settled in the back of his mind, its implications broader than the walls of Windermere ECE center: How does one enkindle the flame of leadership that warms the spirit of both the mentor and the mentee, fostering an environment that transcends mere survival and blooms into holistic prosperity for every individual within its sphere?

LEADERSHIP: THE BEDROCK OF EDUCATIONAL ECOSYSTEMS

Leadership in early childhood education is the cornerstone of program success, particularly within early childhood initiatives such as Head Start, where empowering leaders can foster a culture of growth and stability. Effective leadership support transcends traditional management and enters a realm of transformational practices that ignite passion, drive innovation, and retain high-quality teaching staff. This chapter delves into the anatomy of successful leadership support and its undeniable impact on creating environments where both educators and students flourish.

Understanding the **critical components of leadership support** is essential to constructing a solid foundation for any educational institution. Leadership which harnesses the power of empathy, cognizance, and support, not only shapes the vision and strategy but also forges an inclusive atmosphere that encourages staff retention. It is within such a fabric that teachers feel valued and inspired to extend themselves beyond the basic requirements, significantly improving educational outcomes for children.

Transformational leadership is not just a buzzword; it embodies a crucial shift toward a dynamic where leaders are coaches, cheerleaders, and change agents. Readers will discover the principles of transformational leadership and how such techniques can drastically **reduce turnover rates** among teachers, who often leave due to a lack of support rather than dissatisfaction with the profession itself. The ripple effect of transformational leadership often extends to students who benefit from a stable and engaged teaching workforce.

Strong leadership skills are the lifeblood of a thriving educational environment. This chapter will unpack these skills, highlighting the importance of effective communication, decision-making, and resilience in leadership roles. Early Childhood directors and managers must not only devise strategies but also create an **environment conducive to learning** and teaching. A leader who wields these tools with finesse can foster a climate of mutual respect and shared ambition.

Furthermore, prioritizing the well-being of teachers emerges as a non-negotiable in this dialogue on leadership. Stress, burnout, and dissatisfaction are somber realities in teaching professions, but with robust support from upper management, these challenges can be mitigated or even prevented. Engaging with evidence-based practices that underscore the significance of mental health and work-life balance will bolster not just teacher retention but also the **quality of teaching** delivered.

Drawing on real-world examples, this chapter provides not only a theoretical framework but also a practical guide filled with actionable strategies. These strategies are neither lofty nor idealistic; they are grounded in the realities of educational leadership amidst scarce resources. Through a collaborative spirit, leaders will learn to innovate within constraints, turning potential adversity into a crucible for success.

Given that **continuous learning and development** are central tenets in the field of education, this chapter advocates for a leadership paradigm that is reflective, adaptive, and unafraid of self-transformation. When a leader models growth, it signals to the entire organization that change and personal development are valued and rewarded, thus fostering a culture where everyone is a learner and every moment is an opportunity for growth.

EMPOWERMENT THROUGH INCLUSIVITY AND EQUITY

An inclusive lens of leadership generates a two-fold impact: it caters to a diverse set of needs and promotes equity across the board. This chapter not only values but also integrates diverse perspectives, ensuring that the strategies discussed leave no one behind. By advocating for inclusivity in leadership practices, readers will learn to recognize the unique strengths within their teams, harnessing these to build a resilient, welcoming, and high-functioning workplace.

By the end of the chapter, it will be clear that effective leadership is not a fixed point but a spectrum of adaptive strategies and mindful practices that place the well-being of teachers at the forefront. In advocating for a holistic approach, the reader is invited to embark on a transformational journey marked by innovation, inclusion, and an unwavering commitment to excellence in early childhood education.

Leadership support is a key component in creating an environment where teachers can thrive. Effective leadership provides the guidance, resources, and encouragement necessary for teachers to excel in their roles. To understand the crucial components of effective leadership support in creating a thriving and supportive environment, it's essential to focus on strong leadership skills, transformational leadership, and prioritizing the well-being of teachers.

Strong leadership skills are foundational to creating a supportive environment. Leaders who demonstrate empathy, effective communication, and a clear vision for the organization can foster trust and collaboration among their team. By being able to make tough decisions, provide guidance, and set a positive example, leaders can create a workplace culture that is built on respect and teamwork.

Transformational leadership is a powerful approach that inspires and motivates teachers. This leadership style involves empowering teachers to take ownership of their roles, fostering a culture of innovation, and encouraging professional growth. Transformational leaders are able to communicate a compelling vision, provide individualized support, and recognize the contributions of their team members, fostering a positive and productive work environment.

Prioritizing the well-being of teachers is crucial for creating a supportive and thriving environment. Leaders who prioritize the physical, emotional, and professional well-being of their teachers are, in turn, investing in the success of their students. By offering professional development opportunities, promoting work-life balance, and providing resources for self-care, leaders can ensure that their teachers feel valued and supported.

Understanding the crucial components of effective leadership support is essential for establishing a nurturing and growth-oriented environment for both teachers and students. By prioritizing strong leadership skills, practicing transformational leadership, and valuing the well-being of teachers, leaders can create an environment where teachers can thrive.

Keep reading to learn how these components contribute to creating a supportive and thriving environment for teachers and students. Leadership plays a critical role in the success of any organization, and in the context of early childhood education, it has a direct impact on teacher retention. Transformational leadership is a style of leadership that focuses on inspiring and motivating employees to achieve their full potential. This leadership approach has been shown to have a positive impact on teacher retention and job satisfaction in early childhood settings. By understanding the principles of transformational leadership and its impact on teacher retention, leaders can create an environment where teachers feel supported, valued, and empowered.

One of the key principles of transformational leadership is leading by example. Leaders who embody the values, attitudes, and behaviors they wish to see in their teachers are more likely to gain their respect and trust. When leaders demonstrate a commitment to the well-being and professional development of their teachers, it sets a powerful example that can inspire and motivate the entire team. Another crucial aspect of transformational leadership is the ability to communicate a compelling vision. Effective leaders communicate a clear and compelling vision for the future of the organization and the role that teachers play in achieving that vision. When teachers understand the purpose and impact of their work, they are more likely to feel motivated and engaged.

Empowering teachers is also a fundamental principle of transformational leadership. By giving teachers the autonomy and resources they need to excel in their roles, leaders can foster a sense of ownership and investment in the success of the program. Empowered teachers are more likely to feel satisfied with their work and are more likely to stay in their positions.

Research has shown that transformational leadership has a positive impact on teacher retention in early childhood settings. Transformational leadership is essential in the school setting since this leadership style is constantly looking for methods to create a positive organizational culture. Transformational leaders "build trust and foster collaboration with others" and are "out front advocating change" (Northouse, 2019, pp. 178-179). Grantham-Caston and DiCarlo (2021) found that transformational leaders instill trust in their team members and foster an environment that supports their professional development. Transformational leaders provide individual support and personal attention to each teacher to allow them to reach their goals (Northouse, 2019).

Ultimately, embracing transformational leadership principles can lead to a more supportive and thriving environment for teachers. By practicing leading by example, communicating a compelling vision, and empowering teachers, leaders can create an environment where teachers feel valued, supported, and motivated to stay in their positions.

In the next section, we will delve deeper into the role of strong leadership skills in creating an environment where both teachers and students can thrive.

Strong leadership skills are the foundation upon which a positive educational environment is established. This is particularly true within Head Start programs, where the leadership's abilities directly influence teacher efficacy, job satisfaction, and, ultimately, student success. As educators in leadership positions, one must recognize the weight of their role. Every interaction and decision sets a precedent, affecting the program's culture and operational dynamics.

In the realm of education, particularly early childhood development, strong leadership goes beyond administrative capabilities. It involves emotional intelligence, an understanding of pedagogical strategies, and a commitment to continuous improvement. Leaders must be adept at identifying individual teacher strengths and areas for growth, providing personalized support that fosters both personal and professional development. This investment in teacher growth not only enhances classroom practices but also reinforces teachers' sense of value within the organization.

THE IMPACT OF A NURTURING LEADER

A nurturing leader—one who prioritizes the well-being of their staff—is instrumental in building a supportive work environment. In practice, this might involve regular check-ins, opportunities for teachers to voice concerns, and a system that celebrates achievements. Research has shown that when leaders are approachable and considerate of their staff's needs, job satisfaction increases, and by extension, retention rates improve. This inherently benefits students, who thrive under the guidance of secure and content teachers.

Instituting a culture of professional learning is a critical aspect of strong leadership. Professional development should not be seen as a mere obligation but as an ongoing opportunity for educators to expand their skill sets and refine their teaching methods. Leaders should strive to make these opportunities engaging and relevant, possibly even tailoring them to align with teachers' specific interests or the program's unique needs. This approach demonstrates a commitment to excellence in education and the growth of each team member.

ENCOURAGING REFLECTIVE PRACTICES

Reflection is a vital component of teaching, allowing educators to assess the impact of their work and identify areas for improvement. Effective leaders encourage this reflective practice not just as a solitary activity but as a collaborative process. By fostering an environment where teachers feel comfortable sharing insights and strategies, leaders can facilitate a communal learning experience that elevates the entire program. This collaboration underscores a culture where continuous learning is both expected and respected.

Reflection is a vital component of teaching, allowing educators to assess the impact of their work and identify areas for improvement. Effective leaders encourage this reflective practice not just as a solitary activity but as a collaborative process. By fostering an environment where teachers feel comfortable sharing insights and strategies, leaders can facilitate a communal learning experience that elevates the entire program. This collaboration underscores a culture where continuous learning is both expected and respected.

In the realm of early childhood education, where the stakes are high, **decisive leadership** can make all the difference. This involves making informed decisions promptly, standing firm on educational principles, and navigating challenges with a steadiness that assures both staff and students. A decisive leader instills confidence within their team, providing a stable foundation upon which teachers can develop their teaching philosophies and practices.

THE ROLE OF TECHNOLOGY AND INNOVATION

In today's digitally driven society, leaders must also be at the forefront of incorporating technology and innovation into teaching and learning experiences. This might involve researching the latest educational apps, embracing new digital platforms for teaching, or implementing data-driven strategies to track student progression. By staying abreast of technological advancements, leaders not only enhance the learning environment but also signal to their staff the importance of adaptability and forward-thinking.

Leaders must act as **advocates for equity,** ensuring that all staff and students have access to the resources and support necessary for success. This can involve championing inclusive practices, addressing biases, and working to dismantle systemic barriers that may affect the school community. Through leading by example, leaders can cultivate an atmosphere of fairness and justice within their program.

In essence, robust leadership in educational settings plays a defining role in creating an environment conducive to teacher and student success. This requires a multifaceted approach, blending empathy, innovation, and a constant drive for excellence. By committing to these principles, leaders can foster a community of learning that not only retains its teachers but also empowers them to deliver their best, helping shape the minds and futures of the children they serve.

In the process of implementing effective leadership support, it is imperative to grasp the crucial components that lay the groundwork for a thriving and supportive environment. **Strong leadership** skills are the cornerstone of this foundation, as they empower early childhood directors to navigate the complexities of managing a diverse team while creating an atmosphere conducive to growth and collaboration. By understanding the principles of **transformational leadership**, directors can harness the potential to shape the professional development of their teachers and drive positive changes that elevate the quality of the entire program. Moreover, by prioritizing the well-being of teachers, leaders fulfill a pivotal role in cultivating an environment where both teachers and students can thrive.

With the role of strong leadership skills in mind, it is essential to recognize the tangible impact they have on shaping the culture and effectiveness of an early childhood program. As leaders embrace the principles of transformational leadership, they have the opportunity to nurture a team of educators who are not only well-equipped with the necessary skills but are also driven by a shared vision and sense of purpose. This ethos not only contributes to a supportive environment but also plays a significant role in fostering a strong sense of commitment and motivation among the teachers.

Moving forward, it is crucial for early childhood directors to grasp the exceptional significance of their role in leveraging their leadership skills to create an environment that serves as a catalyst for the well-being and success of both teachers and students. By prioritizing the support, growth, and empowerment of educators, leaders amplify the potential for individual and collective success, thereby setting the stage for an enriching educational experience for all involved. In doing so, they solidify their positions as agents of change, capable of igniting a transformational journey within their program.

Implementing effective leadership support is not just about leading a team; it's about fostering a culture of trust, empowerment, and collaboration. It's about embodying the true essence of leadership and utilizing it as a force for positive change. The diligent implementation of these crucial components will lead to a thriving and supportive environment where the potential for growth and success knows no bounds.

CHAPTER 11

Utilizing Data-Driven Strategies For Teacher Retention

Background

It was an overcast morning in mid-March, the kind where the sky looks like a faded steel canvas, foretelling of rain that stubbornly refuses to fall. Sophia paced the dimly lit hallway of the Little Futures Childcare Program, her lantern jaw set as she passed by classrooms filled with the symphony of young children, their laughter and chatter punctuating her deep contemplations.

As the new Director, she had inherited an exodus of teachers, each one a thread unraveling from the fabric of the school community. The quiet anticipation of change clung to her like the cardigan on her shoulders. She needed to understand the exodus, to halt it, to reverse it—if not for the vitality of the program, then for the futures of the little souls that animated its halls.

Sophia paused by the window, peering out at the small playground with its empty swings swaying in the gentle breeze. She could see the potential of this place, could feel it in her bones, but the retention issue hung over her like Damocles' sword. Her mix of resolve and anxiety was a cocktail she hadn't tasted before.

She retreated to her office, a room that smelled of old books and ambition, and sat behind her desk. Papers adorned with pie charts and bar graphs detailed the attrition numbers, surveys, and exit interviews. Sparse facts that told a story she was still trying to fully comprehend—opportunities for interventions dressed as data points.

A study from a recent educator's journal lay open, the bold title catching her eye: "Data-Driven Strategies for Improving Teacher Retention." Evidence-based decision-making was her stalwart ally. She resolved then to not just be a keeper of records but to read the stories the numbers whispered, each percentage a voice asking for recognition, for a change.

Toying with a pen between her fingers, she thought back to her favorite professor's words, "What gets measured gets managed." Sophia knew she had to do more than just measure. She had to translate the data into tangible solutions—an advocate leveraging facts for the well-being of her staff.

She was snapped out of her reverie by a light knock on the door frame. One of her fledgling teachers, Ms. Grace, stood there, the uncertainty in her eyes reflecting the very challenge Sophia was wrestling with.

"How can I support you, Ms. Grace?" Sophia inquired, her voice steady, hiding the whirlwind inside her. The conversation that ensued was a testament to the gaps she needed to bridge, a personal story adding color to the stark black-and-white of her spreadsheets.

After Ms. Grace left, a newfound determination steeled Sophia's spine. She would craft targeted retention strategies, nurture a supportive culture, foster professional development—and create an environment where teachers, much like the children they taught, could thrive and grow.

The office seemed to brighten a touch as Sophia plotted her course of action. The rain finally began to fall outside, washing the old away. There was work to be done. Why is it that within our grandest challenges often lie the seeds of our greatest triumphs?

HARNESSING THE NUMBERS: THE SECRET TO TEACHER CONTENTMENT

In the tireless quest to cultivate educational excellence in early childhood education programs across the nation, we face the daunting challenge of retaining exceptional teachers. At the crux of this undertaking is the strategic use of data—a beacon guiding leaders through the murky waters of teacher attrition. In this pivotal exploration, directors and professionals operating under the aegis of educational leadership are afforded a lens through which to scrutinize the instrumental role of data-driven strategies in bolstering teacher retention.

The power wielded by numbers cannot be overstated, for it is within the intricate patterns of data that the secrets to teacher satisfaction and longevity lie. By learning **how to leverage data to track and analyze teacher retention metrics**, administrative tacticians can pinpoint with laser precision the factors contributing to their educators' departure. This diagnostic approach sets the stage for administering antidotes in the form of targeted interventions, sabotaging the pitfalls that traditionally plague the teaching profession. Insightful analysis of data thus becomes the cornerstone upon which a formidable foundation for sustainable teacher employment is constructed.

Underpinning this quantitative approach are concrete, evidence-based decisions—actions not born of caprice but of concrete information. Distilled statistics and discernible trends enlighten leadership, informing strategies that mold the educational environment into one where teachers thrive. A commitment to data-driven methodology transcends mere administrivia; it embodies a philosophical shift towards **understanding how data informs targeted interventions**. The elucidation provided by this modus operandi is invaluable, unfurling blueprints for crafting interventions that cater to the needs of educators and, by extension, the children they serve.

The quest for improvement in the realm of teacher retention translates into a triumph for young learners. As such, **recognizing the value of evidence-based decision-making** is not merely an internal adjustment within the confines of administration but a promise to enhance the quality of early education. Each strategic move, guided by data, is a step towards fashioning an ecosystem of learning that captures the dedication and passion of educators well-equipped to inspire young minds. This chapter offers pedagogic leaders a comprehensive roadmap accompanied by proven coordinates, guiding them to the cultivation of retention-rich soil—a necessity for the growth of budding educational landscapes.

PAVING FOUNDATIONS FOR EXCELLENCE: A LEADER'S GUIDE TO PERFORMANCE EVALUATION

ESTABLISHING CLEAR PERFORMANCE STANDARDS

The first stride on the path to exemplary evaluations is the establishment of lucid and quantifiable benchmarks synchronized harmoniously with the vision of each early childhood initiative. By transparently communicating expectations to the faculty, the veil of ambiguity is lifted, unveiling a clear trajectory for professional conduct and pedagogical success.

GATHERING DATA ROUNDTABLE

The subsequent step involves the meticulous collection of data—harvested from classroom observations, educational outcomes, lesson plans, and daily educational discourse—a multivariate approach that encapsulates the multifaceted nature of teaching prowess.

TIMELY AND REFLECTIVE EVALUATIONS

The sequence advances with the scheduling of assessments, a structured interchange around performance—catalyzing reflection, growth, and the crystallization of aspirational goals. Diligence in timing underscores the necessity for this initiative to remain a priority, ensuring the cadence of evaluations remains rhythmic and productive.

CONSTRUCTIVE COMMENDATION AND CRITIQUE

With an emphasis on a strengths-based paradigm, feedback rendered moves beyond critique, transforming into potent fodder for professional flourishing. Precision in recommendations affirms the feedback's tenability and sparks actionable pathways to mastery.

SYNERGY IN GOAL SETTING

In the design of professional horizons, teachers become co-architects, infusing personal ambition with organizational expectations. Goals gain significance through shared vision, enhancing commitment to educational and pedagogical attainment.

BLUEPRINTS FOR SUPPORT

For those navigating steeper paths, individualized blueprints for support emerge as lifelines—detailing routes toward pedagogical fulfillment enabled by strategic support and professional upskilling opportunities.

PROGRESS, SUPPORT, AND ADAPTATION

Active monitoring of advancement couples with steadfast support, recognizing achievement, and responding to challenges—a responsive and dynamic approach nurturing continual progress.

SUMMATIVE REFLECTIONS

Periodic holistic evaluations appraise comprehensive progress, contrasting teacher evolution against the backdrop of community, school, and educational benchmarks. This reflective process calibrates understanding and acknowledges growth.

THE CHRONICLE OF ACHIEVEMENT

Orderly records serve as chronicles of endeavors and benchmarks of progress—imperative for legal compliance and as artifacts of the transformational journey teachers undertake.

CELEBRATING PEDAGOGIC MASTERY

Exemplary teaching deserves celebration. Recognition serves both as validation for the educator's journey and as inspiration, reinforcing the principle that excellence begets excellence in the sacred halls of learning and beyond.

Steering through this articulated process has a definite purpose—to elevate the quality and spirit of teaching within early childhood programs. The conclusive triumph, then, is not merely procedural adherence but a richly woven tapestry of teaching prowess celebrated and perpetuated within the nurturing confines of an empowered educational community.

In the realm of early childhood education, the retention of talented teachers is a crucial factor in the success and well-being of the children they serve. It is essential to understand how to leverage data to track and analyze teacher retention metrics. By doing so, directors and early childhood professionals can gain valuable insights into the underlying causes of attrition and make well-informed decisions to improve teacher retention rates. Tracking and analyzing teacher retention metrics allows for evidence-based decision-making and targeted interventions, which can ultimately lead to a more stable and supportive environment for both educators and students.

Gathering and effectively utilizing data on teacher retention can provide a comprehensive view of the factors contributing to attrition. By tracking metrics such as turnover rates, reasons for leaving, and retention by demographics, directors can identify patterns and trends that may be influencing teacher attrition. **This data can also highlight areas that require attention, such as specific age groups or experience levels of teachers who may be more likely to leave.**

Furthermore, leveraging data can also help in understanding the impact of turnover on the overall quality of education within the program. The ability to quantify the effects of teacher attrition through data analysis can provide a clearer picture of how it affects the children's learning environment and the program's ability to meet educational objectives. **This understanding is crucial for making evidence-based decisions to improve teacher retention and, ultimately, the quality of education provided.**

In addition to providing valuable insights, data-driven strategies can also inform the development of targeted interventions to address the specific causes of teacher attrition. With a clear understanding of the factors contributing to turnover, directors can tailor their retention efforts to directly mitigate these issues. **For example, if data reveals that a high percentage of teachers are leaving due to a lack of career growth opportunities, programs can focus on implementing professional development initiatives and career advancement pathways.**

Data can also be used to evaluate the effectiveness of implemented interventions and ensure that resources are allocated to the areas that will have the most significant impact on teacher retention. By monitoring the outcomes of targeted interventions, programs can adapt and refine their strategies based on real-time feedback, leading to a more proactive and effective approach to teacher retention.

By harnessing the power of data to track and analyze teacher retention metrics, directors and early childhood professionals can gain valuable insights to guide evidence-based decision-making and develop targeted interventions. Let's explore how these data-driven strategies can inform specific interventions to improve teacher retention.

In order to improve teacher retention, it is crucial to understand how data-driven strategies can play a vital role in informing targeted interventions. Data can provide valuable insights into the factors contributing to teacher turnover and help directors and early childhood professionals make informed decisions to address the issues. By harnessing the power of data, it becomes possible to identify specific areas that require intervention, implement evidence-based solutions, and ultimately enhance teacher retention.

Gathering and analyzing data on teacher retention metrics is the first step in utilizing data-driven strategies to inform targeted interventions. By tracking factors such as the length of employment, reasons for leaving, and demographic information, directors and administrators can gain a deeper understanding of the challenges affecting teacher retention within their programs. This data allows for the identification of patterns and trends, enabling informed decision-making regarding interventions that are most likely to have a positive impact.

Through the analysis of data, clear patterns and trends begin to emerge, providing a solid foundation for targeted interventions aimed at improving teacher retention.

Effective data-driven strategies can facilitate evidence-based decision-making by providing a roadmap for targeted interventions. Once the data has been thoroughly analyzed, specific interventions can be tailored to address the root causes of attrition. For example, if the data reveals that a particular demographic group of teachers has higher turnover rates, targeted interventions, such as mentorship programs or professional development opportunities, can be designed to support and retain those educators.

Armed with evidence-based insights, directors and early childhood professionals can implement interventions that are more likely to have a meaningful impact on teacher retention.

By leveraging data-driven strategies to inform targeted interventions, directors and administrators can ensure that their efforts are focused on the areas most likely to yield positive results. This approach allows for the allocation of resources and energy towards initiatives that are evidence-based and have a higher probability of success. Additionally, it creates a more efficient and strategic approach to addressing teacher retention challenges.

Utilizing data-driven strategies provides a solid foundation for targeted interventions, ensuring that efforts are directed toward the most impactful solutions.

In conclusion, data-driven strategies play a crucial role in informing targeted interventions to improve teacher retention. By gathering, analyzing, and leveraging data, directors and early childhood professionals can gain valuable insights that guide evidence-based decision-making and facilitate the implementation of interventions tailored to address the specific challenges contributing to teacher turnover. **Ultimately, by harnessing the power of data, it becomes possible to create a more supportive and thriving environment for both teachers and students.**

DATA-DRIVEN STRATEGIES

HARNESSING THE POWER OF EVIDENCE-BASED DECISION-MAKING

When addressing teacher attrition, the adoption of evidence-based decision-making can be pivotal. This approach ensures that policy adjustments and strategies for retention are not based on anecdotal evidence or intuition but are grounded in concrete data and proven methods. An evidence-based framework begins with gathering quantitative and qualitative data ranging from teacher satisfaction surveys to exit interviews and performance metrics. This data offers invaluable insights into the root causes of turnover and highlights patterns that may not be otherwise apparent.

STRATEGIC DATA UTILIZATION FOR INFORMED INTERVENTIONS

Armed with a clear understanding of teacher turnover dynamics, directors and early childhood professionals are then tasked with interpreting the data to identify the most influential factors affecting retention. This could include aspects such as job satisfaction, support structures, professional development opportunities, and work-life balance. Understanding these elements with granularity allows for focused and strategic interventions. For instance, if data reveals a high correlation between a lack of professional development and teacher departure, programs can tailor resources to bolster training and growth opportunities.

REAL-WORLD APPLICATIONS OF DATA IN TEACHER RETEN-TION

Real-world examples of data driving successful interventions abound. For instance, a program struggling with retention may discover through surveys that teachers feel isolated and unsupported in their roles. By implementing peer-mentoring programs or collaborative planning time, these feelings of isolation can be mitigated, and retention can improve. Such decisions, when based on solid evidence, have a greater chance of yielding positive results because they address specific, identified needs.

CONTINUOUS LEARNING AND IMPROVEMENT

A commitment to continuous improvement is part and parcel of evidence-based decision-making. It recognizes that teacher retention is not a static issue but one that evolves with changes in policy, societal trends, and educational innovations. Continuous learning becomes a strategic advantage, allowing programs to adapt and refine retention strategies as new evidence comes to light. Data-driven approaches thus foster an environment where policies and practices are continually assessed and optimized for efficacy.

INCLUSIVITY AND EQUITY IN DATA-DRIVEN DECISION-MAKING

Inclusivity and equity also play a critical role in data interpretation and subsequent actions. By ensuring that data collection and analysis consider the diverse experiences of all teachers, leaders can create interventions that are fair and beneficial to everyone. For example, minority teachers might face different challenges that contribute to their decisions to leave. Addressing these challenges requires a nuanced understanding that can only come from a comprehensive and inclusive data analysis.

ACTIONABLE STRATEGIES FROM EVIDENCE-BASED INSIGHTS

Directors and early childhood professionals must convert the insights gathered into actionable strategies. Formulating a strategic plan that sets clear objectives, actions, and milestones grounded in evidence is essential for successful implementation. The plan should be transparent, with allocated resources and defined accountability, to ensure that the retention interventions are executed effectively.

COMMUNICATING THE VISION AND PROGRESS

It is equally important to communicate the vision, progress, and successes of any new strategy widely and effectively. Teachers need to understand not only what changes are being made but also how these changes are founded on evidence and how they will benefit the individual and the collective. Effective communication fosters a sense of ownership and engagement in the retention strategies, thus reinforcing their potential impact.

By intertwining data-driven strategies, inclusive analysis, and evidence-based decision-making, Programs can significantly enhance their ability to address teacher attrition. The result is a more stable teaching workforce equipped with the support and resources needed to thrive, ultimately benefiting the children who stand at the heart of every early childhood program's mission.

Leveraging data to track and analyze teacher retention metrics is an indispensable tool for early childhood directors striving to enhance teacher retention in their programs. It provides valuable insights into the factors influencing teacher turnover and empowers decision-makers with evidence-based information to implement targeted interventions. By understanding the patterns revealed through data analysis, **directors can develop informed strategies** to address challenges and nurture a supportive environment for their teaching staff.

Understanding how data-driven strategies can inform targeted interventions to improve teacher retention is pivotal in the quest to build a thriving, supportive environment. Armed with a wealth of data, directors can pinpoint specific areas for improvement and allocate resources effectively. By employing **evidence-based decision-making**, they can utilize strategies tailored to the unique needs of their teaching staff, fostering a culture of support and growth that enables educators to thrive.

Recognizing the value of evidence-based decision-making in addressing teacher attrition in programs is a transformational step toward establishing a sustainable, empowering work environment. When decisions are rooted in data and supported by evidence, they become more likely to yield positive outcomes. Utilizing data to inform decision-making signifies a commitment to **continuous improvement** and a dedication to nurturing teaching talent, ultimately fostering a sense of belonging and purpose among educators.

In summary, the use of data-driven strategies for teacher retention is integral to the success of early childhood programs. Directors who leverage data to inform their decisions and interventions are better equipped to address the challenges of teacher turnover and create a supportive, nurturing environment for their teaching staff. By recognizing the value of evidence-based decision-making, directors can elevate their programs, empower their teachers, and lay the foundation for sustained success.

CHAPTER 12

PROACTIVE AND STRATEGIC APPROACHES TO ADDRESSING TEACHER ATTRITION

BACKGROUND

The early morning sun had begun its ascent, casting a soft glow on the Head Start classroom where Evelyn, the program director, stood amidst a cacophony of cardboard boxes filled with educational toys and resource books. Just outside, the playground lay still, the slides and swings untouched, eagerly awaiting the sound of children's laughter. Inside, the aroma of freshly brewed coffee collided with the crisp scent of new books as Evelyn surveyed her kingdom of potential, her sanctuary of learning.

With every tick of the clock, the sunlight crept further across the checker-patterned floor, edging toward Evelyn's worn shoes. It was in these quiet moments before the day truly began that her mind wandered most. Evelyn was familiar with the turnover battle; it clawed at the very foundations of the program. The truth hung heavily in her thoughts—teacher attrition was not just a nuisance; it was a juggernaut that threatened the continuity and quality of early childhood education. Yet, within her, a strategic plan began to form, inspired by a recent workshop on leadership and teacher retention, her notes from the session spread out on the table like a map to a treasure trove of human potential.

Intermingled with memories of inspiring mentors and past triumphs, doubt occasionally whispered in her ear. Evelyn remembered Marianne, her favorite teacher, whose laughter once filled this very room but who had moved on to a different career due to burnout. The quiet dread of losing another Marianne gripped Evelyn momentarily, yet in that grip, a resilient determination was born. She envisioned a future where her workforce was stable, empowered, and thriving, where the children's educational groundwork was laid with unwavering hands.

The distant sound of a car door closing snapped Evelyn back into the present. Her assistant, Carlos, a pillar of support and a beacon of optimism, walked through the door, his smile an infectious morning greeting. "Ready for the challenge?" he asked, and she nodded, her resolve hardening with every supportive interaction, each one a brick in the fortress she was steadily building against attrition.

Their conversation flowed into the strategies they could implement—mentorship programs, recognition systems, and professional development plans. Each idea brought a spark to Evelyn's eyes, like stars lighting her path through a darkened sky of uncertainty. They spoke of research, evidence-based training, and balancing teacher workloads—each topic a possible thread in the intricate tapestry of making their program an exceptional place to work.

As the hum of activity picked up with the arrival of teachers and children, Evelyn stood as a sentinel of change. She had seen firsthand how strategic initiatives could transform environments within months, igniting a sense of ownership and pride in her staff. In every interaction, she sowed seeds of encouragement, training her gaze on a future where every member of her team felt valued and supported.

Yet, can a program so rich with dreams withstand the harsher truths of constrained resources and external pressures? Will the strategies born of hopeful mornings and fortified with studies and industry savvy prove resilient enough to stem the tide of departure?

NAVIGATING THE HEADWINDS OF TEACHER TURN-OVER

The pervasive issue of teacher attrition within early childhood programs calls for immediate attention and action. **High teacher turnover** not only affects the stability and quality of early childhood education but also imposes a continual strain on resources and morale. It's essential to grasp the significance of adopting a **proactive and strategic approach** to tackle this issue effectively. Grounded in a combination of research, hands-on experiences, and expert insight, this chapter aims to empower directors and early childhood professionals with actionable strategies designed to curb the attrition rates that plague early childhood programs.

In harnessing the transformational power of skilled leadership, we recognize the pivotal role directors play in shaping the work environment. Enhancing the capabilities of these crucial figures must be a cornerstone of any successful retention strategy. Fortified with the right skills, strategies, and insights, directors can foster a workplace that not only attracts but retains high-quality teaching professionals. As such, this chapter not only delivers methods to improve teacher retention but also underscores the sustained impact these strategies can have when applied with intention and vigor.

Turning the tide on teacher attrition requires an in-depth understanding of its causative factors—low pay, inadequate support, intense workload, and deficient communication are but a few. Articulating a clear and insightful analysis of these challenges is paramount. To facilitate this understanding, practical tools, such as targeted worksheets and hands-on tactics, are provided to guide leadership in addressing each contributing factor directly and effectively.

However, knowledge alone isn't transformative — application is key. Therefore, we underscore the trajectory from learning to action. Directors equipped with strategies from this book can expect to see noticeable improvements **within a few months to a year**. This prompt impact contrasts sharply with the often-protracted struggle tied to limited resources and support, marking a considerable advancement in the quest to optimize early childhood environments.

While each chapter of this book serves as a cornerstone, the synthesis of these ideas here crystallizes the journey from identifying problems to implementing solutions. The continuity and cohesion between chapters are vital, ensuring that the reader progresses from understanding the intricate landscape of early educator attrition to sculpting a robust framework for teacher retention and support.

In the spirit of inclusivity and equity, this chapter embraces a collaborative voice, uniting directors, teachers, and stakeholders in a shared vision. By promoting dialogue and valuing diverse perspectives, **early childhood programs can become a beacon of growth and development**—for the children they serve, the teachers they employ, and the communities they enrich.

The journey toward change is not solitary; it is a dynamic and collective effort marked by continuous learning and professional development. As readers navigate the rich insights offered, they are encouraged to view each strategy not as a remedy in isolation but as part of an integrated and systemic approach to creating high-performing early childhood programs. The empowerment of directors and early childhood professionals is not an end—it is a catalyst for sustained transformation, setting in motion a cycle of improvement that extends far beyond the confines of individual classrooms.

A proactive and strategic approach is essential for effectively addressing high teacher attrition in early childhood programs. Understanding the significance of these approaches is crucial in implementing sustainable solutions that can significantly impact teacher retention and leadership support. By adopting a proactive stance, directors and early childhood professionals can identify potential issues before they escalate, thereby mitigating the impact of teacher attrition on the overall effectiveness of the program. Additionally, a strategic approach allows for the development and implementation of targeted initiatives that align with the specific needs and challenges faced by teachers and administrators. This intentional focus on problem-solving enhances the effectiveness of efforts to reduce attrition and improve overall program quality.

Recognizing the need for proactive measures is the first step in ensuring the long-term success of an early childhood program.

Strategic actions informed by data and research are essential for addressing the root causes of teacher attrition. A comprehensive understanding of the contributing factors to attrition enables the development of targeted interventions that can directly impact teacher retention. By leveraging data-driven strategies, directors and early childhood professionals can allocate resources and implement initiatives that directly address the underlying issues leading to attrition. These targeted interventions can lead to immediate improvements in teacher satisfaction and commitment to the program, laying the groundwork for sustained progress in reducing turnover rates.

A strategic approach empowers program leaders to actively and effectively respond to the challenges of teacher attrition.

Furthermore, a proactive and strategic approach fosters a culture of continuous improvement within early childhood programs. By consistently evaluating and refining retention and support strategies, program leaders can ensure that their efforts remain aligned with the evolving needs of their staff. This ongoing commitment to improvement not only addresses the immediate challenges of teacher attrition but also creates a supportive environment that encourages professional growth and development. This, in turn, enhances the overall quality of education and care provided to the children in the program.

Embracing a proactive and strategic approach sets the stage for sustained success and growth.

Understanding the value of these proactive and strategic approaches is crucial for directors and early childhood professionals seeking to create a thriving and supportive environment that retains top teaching talent. Let's explore the importance of empowering leaders with the right skills and strategies to improve teacher retention.

Recognize the importance of empowering directors and early childhood professionals with the right skills and strategies to improve teacher retention.

Empowering directors and early childhood professionals with the right skills and strategies is crucial in improving teacher retention in early childhood programs. By providing them with the necessary tools and knowledge, they can create a supportive and thriving environment where teachers feel valued, supported, and motivated to stay.**Equipping these leaders with effective communication skills, conflict resolution techniques, and leadership development programs can have a profound impact on the overall retention rates within the program.**

Communication skills are fundamental in fostering positive relationships and creating an open environment where teachers feel heard and understood. Directors who are adept at active listening, providing constructive feedback, and communicating effectively can build trust and rapport, which are essential for retaining teachers. Additionally, conflict resolution techniques are invaluable in addressing challenges in a constructive and respectful manner, ultimately contributing to a healthier work environment and higher retention rates.

Moreover, investing in leadership development programs for directors and early childhood professionals can have a transformational effect on the entire program. By honing their leadership skills, they can inspire and motivate their teams, set clear expectations, and provide the necessary support for teachers to thrive. These programs can also cultivate a culture of continuous learning and professional growth, which is essential for retaining top teaching talent.

It's also important to provide directors and early childhood professionals with strategies for recognizing and addressing burnout among teachers. This can include initiatives that promote self-care, stress management, and work-life balance. By proactively addressing burnout, leaders can create a more sustainable and supportive work environment that contributes to improved teacher retention. Furthermore, offering professional development opportunities and career advancement pathways can incentivize teachers to stay within the program. This can include access to training, workshops, and mentorship programs that support their professional growth and provide a clear trajectory for their career within the program.

Ultimately, by empowering directors and early childhood professionals with the right skills and strategies, programs can establish a culture of support, growth, and appreciation. This empowerment sets the stage for improved teacher retention, ultimately benefiting both the educators and the children they serve.

IMPLEMENT TACTICAL MEASURES FOR IMMEDIATE IMPACT

Speed is a critical factor when addressing teacher attrition in early childhood programs. It is possible to enact positive change swiftly by implementing tactical measures specifically tailored to the most pressing challenges. Immediate steps could include enhanced professional development opportunities, mentorship programs, and regular feedback mechanisms — all of which can contribute to a more supportive environment and demonstrate a commitment to teacher growth. Each of these initiatives, once in place, serves to empower educators and can lead to quick wins that solidify trust and buy-in from staff.

GATHER AND APPLY ACTIONABLE DATA

Data-driven decisions are essential in tailoring strategies to the unique needs of an institution. By conducting regular surveys and exit interviews, programs can gather invaluable insights into the reasons behind teacher turnover. Acting on this feedback, directors can pinpoint areas for improvement and initiate targeted interventions. It is vital to ensure these efforts are followed by an analysis of their effectiveness, allowing for agile adjustments and fine-tuning. When teachers see their concerns being taken seriously and acted upon, it fosters a sense of inclusion and value that can greatly enhance retention.

ELEVATE LEADERSHIP CAPACITIES

Developing strong leadership within a program is a fundamental strategy for alleviating high attrition. Effective leaders inspire confidence, foster a shared vision, and create a culture of collaboration and professional fulfillment. Leadership training for directors and the incorporation of leadership pathways for teachers are tactics that can be realized relatively swiftly yet have lasting impacts. As teachers perceive avenues for career progression and feel supported by adept leaders, their commitment to an organization can solidify, thus mitigating the risk of turnover.

ENHANCE COMPENSATION STRUCTURES

While structural changes to compensation might not be as quick to deploy, even steps toward improving the financial recognition of teachers can have a quick effect on morale. By exploring alternative funding, grants, and partnership opportunities, programs can work towards offering more competitive wages and benefits. When teachers observe sincere efforts to improve their financial well-being, it can serve as a powerful motivator for them to stay with the organization while longer-term solutions are put into place.

ENCOURAGE A CULTURE OF WELL-BEING

Inculcating a culture that prioritizes the well-being of educators is an indispensable strategy that can be acted upon with immediacy. Simple measures like providing wellness resources or establishing protocols for a more balanced work-life dynamic can happen rapidly. These initiatives not only help in alleviating burnout but also demonstrate to teachers that their personal health and happiness are valued by their employers. Over time, this can translate into increased job satisfaction and loyalty.

INVEST IN A SUPPORTIVE INFRASTRUCTURE

Investment in infrastructure — whether that be physical resources or supportive systems — can also play a significant role in reducing teacher attrition. For example, providing teachers with access to quality teaching materials and tech support can remove day-to-day frustrations, thereby allowing them to focus on what they do best: teaching. Such upgrades can typically be rolled out in a short period, and their benefits can be immediately felt by staff, contributing to an overall more positive work environment.

AMPLIFY VOICES THROUGH SHARED GOVERNANCE

Creating channels for teacher input in decision-making processes doesn't require a multi-year overhaul; it can begin with setting up regular staff meetings or advisory committees. By incorporating teacher voices into the governance of the program, you inherently value their expertise and viewpoints. This form of shared governance helps to build a cooperative community where the teachers feel respected and integral to the program's direction and success, potentially reducing the feeling of helplessness that can lead to burnout and attrition.

FOSTER COMMUNITY CONNECTIONS

Finally, building stronger relationships with the local community can enhance a sense of belonging and support for teachers. Engaging in community events, forming partnerships with local businesses, and involving family members in certain aspects of the program can all be initiated quickly. These connections not only enrich the educational environment for the children but also provide a network of support and recognition for teachers, further embedding them within the fabric of the program and community.

By addressing these areas with urgency and focus, substantial progress can be made in confronting teacher attrition. Early victories not only boost morale but can also set a precedent for continued improvements. It is through these concerted, tactical efforts can pave the way for a more robust, sustainable future, keeping the welfare and retention of teachers at the forefront of their mission.

In this chapter, we've explored the significance of proactive and strategic approaches to addressing high teacher attrition rates. We've emphasized the importance of empowering directors and early childhood professionals with the right skills, tactics, and strategies to improve teacher retention and leadership support within a relatively short timeframe. By understanding the contributing factors to teacher attrition and implementing effective tactics, positive change can be realized, mitigating common challenges and fostering a supportive environment for early childhood educators.

Through this book, we've delved into the numerous factors contributing to high teacher attrition, ranging from low pay and heavy workloads to inadequate support and poor communication. By equipping readers with strategies and worksheets to address each of these factors, we have provided a comprehensive understanding of the challenges at hand and the means to address them.

The transformational power of learning and development cannot be overstated. By harnessing the strategies and tools outlined in this book, early childhood directors have the potential to bring about significant change within their programs. The positive impact of proactive and strategic efforts to improve teacher retention can be realized in as little as a few months to a year, enabling the creation of a thriving, supportive environment for both educators and children.

As we conclude this chapter and the book as a whole, remember that the proactive and strategic approaches outlined here are not merely theoretical concepts. They are practical, actionable steps aimed at effecting meaningful change in your program. With diligence, dedication, and the application of the strategies provided, it is within your power to create a work environment that supports, nurtures, and retains top teaching talent, ultimately benefiting the children and families in your care.

The journey toward transforming early childhood programs through improved teacher retention and leadership support is an ongoing one, but with the right tools and mindset, it is a journey that holds the promise of lasting, positive change.

So, take the insights and strategies offered in this book and start your journey toward a more vibrant and supportive early childhood program today. Your commitment to empowering and retaining top teaching talent will lay the foundation for a brighter future for both your educators and the children they serve.

A GUIDING LIGHT TO TEACHER RETENTION AND LEADERSHIP EXCELLENCE

As we draw the curtains on our journey through the labyrinth of challenges and opportunities within the environment, it's imperative to acknowledge the transformational power of the knowledge we've shared. Emanating from a wealth of experience, research, and real-world applications, the insights within these pages serve as a beacon for directors and early childhood professionals striving for excellence in their programs. **The essence of this book lies in its foundational belief that with the right strategies, dedication, and support, overcoming the hurdles of teacher attrition is not just a possibility but a reality.**

Navigating through the multifaceted landscape of early childhood education, you've been equipped with **tools and strategies** that are not merely theoretical but steeped in practicality. They promise actionable insights that can be applied to the unique contexts of your programs. From building a culture of appreciation and respect to empowering educators with professional development opportunities, the themes we've explored are your allies in the mission to retain top talent.

Recapitulating the core pillars, we've delved into the significance of responsive leadership, the cultivation of a supportive community, and the paramount importance of fostering a work environment that values and uplifts every member. By applying the methodologies and insights gleaned, you're not only embarking on a path to diminishing attrition rates but also, perhaps more crucially, enlightening the lives of the educators and children within your programs.

Empowering you to put these insights into action, it's encouraged to utilize the worksheets and strategies provided as a starting point to tailor solutions that resonate with your unique challenges and opportunities. Be open to adaptation and innovate with the content to suit your evolving needs. Remember, transformation is a journey, not a destination, and continuous improvement is the key to enduring success.

In acknowledging the **limitations of this work**, it's vital to understand that while extensive, the strategies and insights provided may not encompass the entirety of the challenges faced in every unique context. The landscape of early childhood education is ever-evolving, demanding ongoing research, adaptation, and creativity in problem-solving approaches.

Thus, **your call to action** is clear. Leverage the knowledge, strategies, and inspiration gleaned from this book to initiate tangible changes in your programs. Be the change agent that not only transforms the trajectory of your teachers' professional lives but also enriches the learning experiences of the children who are the future.

Let this book not be a conclusion but a commencement—a spark igniting the flame of dedication and innovation within you. As you turn the pages of this chapter in your professional journey, remember that the power to effectuate change resides within you. **Together, let's pave the way for a brighter, more resilient future for early childhood programs, where every educator feels valued, supported, and empowered to nurture the minds and hearts of our youngest learners.**

In parting, always remember the words of Margaret Mead, "Never doubt that a small group of thoughtful, committed citizens can change the world. Indeed, it's the only thing that ever has." Let this be a clarion call to action, to not only dream of a better future for early childhood education but to be the architects of its realization.

"Never doubt that a small group of thoughtful, committed citizens can change the world. Indeed, it's the only thing that ever has." - Margaret Mead.

CHAPTER 13

WORKBOOK & REFLECTIONS

BACKGROUND

Beyond theory lies practical application. Our interactive workbook is a series of exercises designed to provoke thought, enhance understanding, and enable professional growth. Reflections, application of theories, and strategic planning for a program's future are all included, transforming the read into a personalized blueprint for success.

CENTER DIRECTOR'S REFLECTIVE WORKSHEET ON JOB SATISFACTION

Are you ready to dive deep into the heart of your center's overall satisfaction and really make some waves? I've crafted this empowering worksheet to help you reflect on the job satisfaction within your center. This isn't just any worksheet; it's your personal compass to navigating and enhancing the well-being of your amazing team!

Section 1: Understanding Teacher Efficacy and Trust

Reflect on Trust: When was the last time you acknowledged your team's efforts in a way that boosted their trust in you and the center's mission?

Gauge Efficacy: On a scale from 1 to 10, how empowered do your teachers feel to lead their classrooms toward success?

Section 2: Assessing Organizational Support

Evaluate Support Systems: How does your center provide personalized support to its educators? Outline a recent scenario where you delivered exceptional support.

Organizational Health Check: What feedback have you received from staff about the support they receive? Any areas for improvement?

Section 3: Fostering Strong Coworker Relationships

Building Connections: Share a success story of a teamwork initiative that really brought cohesiveness to the group.

Conflict Resolution: Describe your approach to resolving conflicts among staff. How can you improve this process to bolster job satisfaction?

Section 4: Balancing Pressures and Satisfaction

Managing Time and Pressure: How do you ensure that your teachers aren't overloaded and can maintain a healthy work-life harmony?

Spotlight on Satisfaction: What innovative method have you implemented lately to raise job satisfaction levels?

Remember, as a dedicated center director, your intuition and actions are key to crafting an environment that not only educates but energizes and engages every single educator! Let's get to work on making your center a beacon of job satisfaction! Go ahead, take this worksheet, and turn it into action — because together, we can sculpt an extraordinary educational experience!

JOB SATISFACTION CHALLENGE WORKSHEET FOR CENTER DIRECTORS

It's time to roll up your sleeves and dive into the heart of your education center. This worksheet is your secret weapon to unlock the highest levels of job satisfaction in your team. Together, we're going to identify not just challenges but opportunities – because that's what they really are – to elevate morale and cultivate a thriving work environment.

Part 1: Identifying Challenges

Current Pain Points: What daily obstacles are dampening your team's spirit? List them here, and let's tackle them head-on!

Illegitimate Tasks: Are there tasks that don't align with your team's roles? Shine a light on them – we're here to make everyone feel valued for the true work they do.

Recognition and Rewards: Is the team feeling seen? Jot down how often you celebrate their achievements – small or big, every win counts!

Part 2: Actionable Strategies

Team Engagement: What initiatives can we introduce to involve the team in decision-making? They're the backbone of your center, and their voice is powerful!

Skill Development: Where can we provide more growth and learning opportunities? Each team member has potential just waiting to be unleashed.

Work Environment: What changes can make your center a beacon of positivity and productivity? Dream big, and let's make it happen.

Part 3: Implementation Plan

Short-term Goals: Identify quick wins that can immediately boost the team's morale. We're in the business of making positive changes, and the time is now!

Long-term Vision: Outline goals for the future that align with job satisfaction and happiness. Together, we're paving the path to a joyous and fulfilling workplace.

Taking the time to complete this worksheet is already a testament to your dedication. You've got this! Now, let's turn those challenges into stepping stones for success and make your center the envy of educational excellence across the globe!

Remember, every challenge is an opportunity to grow stronger, and together, we're unstoppable!

PROFESSIONAL DEVELOPMENT PLANNING WORK-SHEET

Let's ignite the spark of continuous learning within our team!

Hello Transformative Leaders! Are you ready to elevate and empower your amazing team of educators? This Professional Development Planning Worksheet is crafted to assist you, the stalwart champions of education, in sculpting an enriching environment where professional growth is not just an option but a thrilling adventure!

Educator Empowerment Plan

Identify Growth Areas

Reflect on the in-service and pre-service growth areas needed for the team. List them down:

Pinpoint the individual strengths of your staff. How can these be further cultivated? Write your ideas here:

Set Clear Objectives

What are the key outcomes you envision after the professional development period? Detail these targets:

How will you measure success? Define your yardstick:

Map Out the Opportunities

Research and list upcoming workshops, seminars, and training sessions:

Draft potential on-site training with experienced mentors. Who could shine in leading these? Brainstorm:

Allocation of Resources

Budget plays a pivotal role – plan your financial resources to ensure these opportunities are feasible:

Chronicle any material needs for professional development. Let's leave no stone unturned:

Implementation Timeline

Craft a timeline that radiates ambition but respects the balance:

Launch Phase: When will the new professional development initiatives start?

Momentum Phase: Outline checkpoints to review progress and maintain energy:

Celebration Phase: When we triumph, let's celebrate growth and success! Plan this well-deserved moment: _____

Remember, shaping a bright future in early childhood education begins with investing in our educators. Let's roll up our sleeves and dive into this journey together – your commitment and foresight can transform the landscape of learning!

Together, we are unstoppable!

Let's break these tasks down into manageable steps and make professional development a powerful, exhilarating reality for our team. Go ahead, take the reins, and let's make magic happen!

REFLECTIVE TEACHER WELL-BEING WORKSHEET

Hey Superstars, it's **YOUR** time to shine bright in the reflective mirror of self-discovery and evoke the change you were born to make in the education world! This isn't just another form—think of it as your personal stress-detox booth, your launchpad to a happier, healthier you in our esteemed teaching community. Let's dive deep together and identify what's cranking up the pressure so we can blast it off into space where it belongs!

Section 1: Charting Your Stress Universe

Overall Stress Levels: Think about your week—are you surfing on serene waves or feeling the typhoon's hit? Scale it from 1 (Zen-like calmness) to 10 (I need a space suit!).

Stress Comet Crashers: List down any asteroid-sized stresses that make an unexpected entry in your week. What's throwing you off balance?

Star Stressors: Pick out the daily stress twinkle stars that are consistently part of your galaxy. They may seem small, but they add up!

Section 2: Curriculum Conundrums

Curriculum Compatibility Check: Does the curriculum feel like a well-fitting spacesuit, or is it like wearing a suit made for a Martian? Share your compatibility story.

Lesson Planning Lift-off: Are your lesson plans soaring high, or are emergency landings the norm? Describe the ease or challenges of your lesson planning journey.

Resource Recharge Station: Do you feel like you've got a galaxy of resources at your fingertips, or is the supply as scarce as water on the moon? List the resources you need more of.

Section 3: The Stellar Self-Efficacy Sphere

Teaching Superpowers Assess: I know you've got superpowers—how often are you able to flex them in the classroom? Give specific examples of when you've felt most empowered and effective.

Kryptonite Discovery: Sometimes, even superheroes find their kryptonite. What areas in teaching weaken your confidence, and how might we armor up against them?

Confidence Constellations: Draw a constellation representing the strength of your self-efficacy in the classroom. More stars indicate stronger self-efficacy—what does your constellation look like?

-Wrap-Up Reflection-

With an exuberant heart and the wisdom of a thousand classrooms, jot down your thoughts, feelings, and lightbulb moments from this activity. Remember, you're not just filling out a worksheet; you're carving the path to a more balanced, fulfilling career in education. Together, let's harness our collective energy to not just reach for the stars—but to become them.

Note to Center Director: A diligent review of this worksheet will help you steer our educational spaceship in a direction that supports, nurtures, and uplifts our phenomenal teaching crew. Armed with this knowledge, we can boldly venture into a universe where every educator feels supported and every classroom shines with possibility.

 This worksheet is a beacon guiding you through the cosmic challenge of stress and self-efficacy in teaching. Fill it with courage, use it with enthusiasm, and remember—I'm right here beside you, cheering on your meteoric rise to legendary educator status! Let's transform stress into stellar success!

HOW TO BUDGET FOR TEACHING STAFF PAY RAISES: A STEP-BY-STEP WORKSHEET

Hello, incredible leaders of education! You are the unsung heroes sculpting the future, one brilliant young mind at a time. I know you're not just a director; you're the cornerstone of a thriving educational community, and that's why you understand that happy teachers foster success in the classroom. So, let's dive into the heart of making a positive change — giving your dedicated teachers the pay raise they deserve. Ready to empower your team and ignite even more passion for education? Let's do this!

1. Assess the Current Financial Landscape:

I believe in you, and you should, too! Let's get fiscal but also visionary because our teachers aren't just a line in a budget — they're the heartbeat of education. Let's work towards those pay increases and witness the thriving educational environment we know we can create together! (Place this worksheet in a common area and encourage all stakeholders to provide input. Your collective wisdom is the wellspring of transformative solutions!)

o What is your current budget for salaries?
o What financial resources are available that could be adjusted or repurposed for increases in pay?

2. Explore Additional Funding Opportunities:

o Are there grants available that focus on educational staff development?
o Can you collaborate with community partners for sponsorship or funding initiatives?

3. Determine Pay Increase Goals:

o What is the ideal pay increase percentage you aim to provide?
o How will these increases benefit the teachers, the students, and the overall learning environment?

4. Calculate the Total Cost of Proposed Raises:

o Determine the additional annual cost of the desired raises.
o Is this a sustainable figure when considering the budget year over year?

5. Design a Phased Plan for Implementation:

o If immediate full raises are not feasible, what is a realistic timeline for phased pay increases?

o How will you communicate these changes to your staff to ensure transparency and maintain morale?

6. Review & Adjust Budget to Accommodate Raises:

o What current expenses can be reduced or eliminated without compromising the quality of education?

o How can you optimize operational efficiency to redirect savings toward salaries?

7. Set Up a Monitoring and Review Procedure:

o How will you track the impact of these pay increases on staff retention and job satisfaction?

o What metrics will you use to assess the success of the investment in your staff?

8. Get Creative with Non-Monetary Benefits:

o Can you offer additional professional development opportunities?

o What about work-life balance enhancements like flexible scheduling or wellness programs?

REFLECTIVE WORKSHEET: ASSESSING SOCIAL SUPPORT WITHIN YOUR TEAM

Hey there, amazing Center Directors! Let's dive deep into the heart of our educational community – yes, I'm talking about our incredible staff, the superheroes in the classrooms! I've crafted a simple yet powerful reflective worksheet for you. This is your tool to ensure every member of your team feels the strong, supportive embrace of your leadership. Are you ready to become the champion of social support? Let's do this!

Section 1: Self-Reflection

• **Genuine Connection:** Do I know my teachers beyond their professional roles? Reflect on moments you've taken to connect personally with your staff.

• **Open-Door Policy:** Have I created an environment where my teachers feel comfortable sharing their challenges? Note instances when staff have sought support and how it was handled.

Section 2: Observation Checklist

• **Team Interactions:** Observe your staff during breaks and collaborative moments. Are they comfortable, open, and supportive with each other?

• **Support in Action:** Identify situations where your leadership team provided support to a staff member. What form did it take, and how effective was it?

Section 3: Surveying Team Satisfaction

• **Ask for Feedback:** Conduct anonymous surveys asking staff to rate the level of support they feel and where they might need more help.

• **Regular Check-Ins:** How often do I schedule one-on-one meetings to talk about my teachers' well-being?

Section 4: Action Plan

• **Sketch an Enhancement Strategy:** Using your observations and survey results, draft up a plan to improve social support.

• **Development Resources:** What professional development opportunities can you offer to reinforce self-regulation and coping skills?

Section 5: Follow-Up and Adaptation

• **Measure Improvement:** Set goals and timelines to assess progress in social support.

• **Stay Open to Change:** Be willing to adapt your strategies based on ongoing feedback and results.

Remember, a flourishing team is the bedrock of an exceptional educational experience for our young learners. It's not just about noble intentions; it's about creating actionable, sustained change—because you value each team member. You've got this, you're not just building a team; you're nurturing a family. Now, let's bolster our social support and watch our educational community soar to incredible heights!

CLASSROOM OBSERVATION CHECKLIST FOR CENTER DIRECTORS

Alright, team leaders! This is where we shift gears from great to phenomenal. Strap in because I've cooked up a classroom observation checklist that's your new best friend. Use it to spot the superstars, to find those moments of pure educational gold!

• **Engagement and Enthusiasm:** Is the teacher's passion for teaching evident? Do they make every lesson feel like an adventure waiting to happen?

• **Innovation in Action:** How does the educator integrate creative teaching strategies to spark curiosity? Are they using technology as a superpower to transport kids to new worlds of knowledge?

• **Student Participation:** Are the students actively involved? Check if every young mind is not just a spectator but a vibrant contributor to the learning journey.

• **Classroom Management:** Observe the flow of the classroom. Is the teacher a maestro, artfully conducting the symphony of learning while keeping the class in harmony?

• **Inclusivity:** Does the teacher accommodate diverse learning needs? Keep an eye out for the magic makers who ensure that no child is left behind.

• **Feedback and Improvement:** Notice the response to student questions and challenges. Is the teacher a builder, turning every mistake into a steppingstone for growth?

• **Professionalism:** Is there a sense of mutual respect between teachers and students? Look for the leaders who wear their hearts on their sleeve and their professionalism as their badge of honor.

Make notes, my friends, and remember, we are on the hunt for those who are not just filling minds with knowledge but are filling hearts with dreams! Take this checklist as your treasure map as you navigate through the classrooms. Let's unveil the educators who are the champions of tomorrow today!

SCHOOL CLIMATE SURVEY

Early Childhood Program School Climate Survey

Hey there, extraordinary educators and remarkable caregivers! It's time to make our voices heard and create a climate that's as vibrant and nurturing as the imaginations of our tiny tots. Together, we can craft an early childhood program that's not just good, but oh-wow-I-can't-believe-this-is-real great!

Please take a few magical moments to complete this survey. Your insights are the paint to our canvas – let's create a masterpiece for our children!

1. Safe and Caring Environment:

I feel like a superhero in a safe fortress:

Do you feel your environment is as safe as can be, allowing both the little ones and you to focus on the joy of learning?

A blanket of care and understanding:

How well do you believe our program responds to the emotional needs of each cherished child?

2. Quality of Facilities:

Our treasure trove for learning:

Rate the quality of our facilities. Are the playgrounds, classrooms, and restrooms serving as launchpads to learning and discovery?

3. Relationships and Collaboration:

A fellowship of learning wizards:

How powerful is the collaboration between staff and parents? Are we all in this thrilling quest together?

4. Support for Growth and Learning:

Fertilizer for growing minds:

Do you feel equipped with resources and training opportunities to keep on growing, thriving, and being the guides our children deserve?

5. Professional Respect:

• Champions of tomorrow, celebrated today:

Is the dedication and expertise of our staff recognized and celebrated? We're in this for the high-fives and heartfelt thank-yous that fuel us!

6. Feedback for the Journey Ahead:

• Charting the course with stars in our eyes:

How can we, as a team, improve our program? Your suggestions are the stars we navigate by, leading us to new horizons!

Take a little leap, take this survey, and together, let's continue to make our early childhood program a magical place where curiosity blooms and every child feels like they can reach for the stars!

Your passionate contribution to this survey is a cornerstone to building a thriving, joyful, and inclusive future for our children. I'm counting on you, dear change-maker, to share your perspective and help steer our ship to the land of excellence. Let's do this – for the love of learning and the love of our children!

SAMPLE INTERVIEW QUESTIONS

I know you've got the spark, the zeal, the unwavering commitment to education that we so cherish! So, let's dive right in with interview questions that aren't just cookie-cutter formalities but true catalysts for discovering the beating heart behind those hopeful eyes. We're not just looking for teachers; we're seeking out world-changers and dream-makers – the ones who will shape tomorrow with every story they tell and every question they ask!

Please take a few magical moments to complete this survey. Your insights are the paint to our canvas – let's create a masterpiece for our children!

"Paint me a picture of your ideal classroom. How do you bring that vibrant picture to life within our walls?" Let's get a glimpse into their world, where imagination meets reality, and how they plan to sprinkle that magic into our learning spaces.

"Can you share an experience where you turned a challenge into a triumphant learning opportunity?" It's about spotting those who see the silver lining, who transform 'Oops!' into 'Aha!' moments that kids remember forever.

"In your words, what's the secret ingredient to fostering a love of learning at such a tender age?" We're after that secret sauce, the one that makes their teaching flavor irresistible to curious young minds.

"Describe how you've tailored your teaching methods to accommodate different learning styles." Because we know every child is a unique puzzle, we need educators who are puzzle masters – adept at fitting the right pieces together.

"Can you tell me about a time your initiative had a profound impact on a student or a classroom?" We want those with a track record of not just doing but changing the game – leaving imprints of inspiration wherever they go.

"Can you tell me about a time when you had a challenging experience with a co-worker or a person in a leadership position?" We want those who have found a way to resolve the situation.

My friends, let's not just listen to their answers; let's hear their stories, feel their passion, and see the determination in their eyes. We're building an army of heart-driven educators, and every question is our chance to unearth those gems. Let's do this!

REFLECTION 1

Reflection is a window to observing our growth and understanding our challenges. What can I do as a director to provide support to my staff?

REFLECTION 2

Reflection is a window to observing our growth and understanding our challenges. How can I support my staff during planning time?

REFLECTION 3

Reflection is a window to observing our growth and understanding our challenges. How can I support my staff with dealing with challenging behaviors?

REFLECTION 4

Reflection is a window to observing our growth and understanding our challenges. What can I do differently to ensure my staff are receiving proper training? How can I ensure that the training is specific to the needs of my staff?

REFLECTION 5

Reflection is a window to observing our growth and understanding our challenges. Are my onboarding procedures detailed enough to provide new staff with the necessary information and training to be successful? How long is my training before staff enter the classroom? Am I creating a disaster or preventing one?

REFLECTION 6

Reflection is a window to observing our growth and understanding our challenges. If I am an executive director, how am I supporting my center directors? What can I do differently to provide more support?

REFLECTION 7

Reflection is a window to observing our growth and understanding our challeng-es. Am I creating excessive workloads for my staff? What can I do to alleviate some of the workload?

REFLECTION 8

Reflection is a window to observing our growth and understanding our challenges. Am I creating too many meetings? Can some of the messages be passed through email?

REFLECTION 9

Reflection is a window to observing our growth and understanding our challenges. How can I implement mental health consultants or services for my staff? Can I create a community partnership for a mental health consultant?

REFLECTION 10

Reflection is a window to observing our growth and understanding our challenges. What can I do to create a space for mental health?

REFLECTION 11

Reflection is a window to observing our growth and understanding our challenges. Do I have an authentic relationship with my staff? If not, what can I do to create one?

REFLECTION 12

Reflection is a window to observing our growth and understanding our challenges. Am I transparent and accessible to my staff? If not, what can I do to change this?

REFLECTION 13

Reflection is a window to observing our growth and understanding our challenges. Do I truly know the needs and wants of my staff? If not, what can I do to change this?

REFLECTION 14

Reflection is a window to observing our growth and understanding our challenges. What tools can I utilize to increase communication and receive authentic
feedback without judgment?

REFERENCES:

Apostel, E., Syrek, C. J., & Antoni, C. H. (2018). Turnover intention as a response to illegitimate tasks: The moderating role of appreciative leadership. International Journal of Stress Management, 25(3), 234–249. https://doi.org/10.1037/str0000061

Barnett, W. S. (2002). The battle overhead starts: What the research shows. Presentation at a Science and Public Policy Briefing Sponsored by the Federation of Behavioral, Psychological, and Cognitive Sciences. https://www.researchgate.net/publication/247789953_The_Battle_Over_Head_Start_What_the_Research_Shows

Bass, B. M. (1985). Leadership and performance beyond expectations. Free Press.

Bell, L. (2021, October). How can we reduce turnover among early childhood educators? Pay them more, a study finds. EducationNC. https://www.ednc.org/2021-10-04 turnover-retention-early-childhood-educators-better-pay-wage-study-supplement/

Bridges, M., Fuller, B., Huang, D. S., & Hamre, B. K. (2011). Strengthening the early childhood workforce: How wage incentives may boost training and job stability. Early Education & Development, 22(6), 1009–1029. https://doi.org/10.1080/10409289.2010.514537

Brill, S., & McCartney, A. (2008). Stopping the revolving door: Increasing teacher retention. Politics & Policy, 36(5), 750–774. https://doi.org/10.1111/j.1747-1346.2008.00133.x

Bryman, A. (1999). Leadership in organizations. In Managing organizations: Current issues (1st ed., p. 32). SAGE Publications Ltd. https://doi.org/https://www.google.com/books/edition/_/z8fVq1_0W4QC?hl=en&gbpv=1

Bullough, R. V., Hall-Kenyon, K. M., & MacKay, K. (2012). Head start teacher well-being: \ Implications for policy and practice. Early Childhood Education Journal, 40(6), 323–331. https://doi.org/10.1007/s10643-012-0535-8

Carson, R. L., Baumgartner, J. J., Ota, C. L., Kuhn, A., & Durr, A. (2016). An ecological momentary assessment of burnout, rejuvenation strategies, job satisfaction, and quitting intentions in childcare teachers. Early Childhood Education Journal, 45(6), 801–808. https://doi.org/10.1007/s10643-016-0831-9

Cassidy, D. J., Lower, J. K., Kintner-Duffy, V. L., Hegde, A. V., & Shim, J. (2011). The day-to-day reality of teacher turnover in preschool classrooms: An analysis of classroom context and teacher, director, and parent perspectives. Journal of Research in Childhood Education, 25(1), 1–23. https://doi.org/10.1080/02568543.2011.533118

Collie, R. J., Shapka, J. D., & Perry, N. E. (2012). School climate and social-emotional learning: Predicting teacher stress, job satisfaction, and teaching efficacy. Journal of Educational Psychology, 104(4), 1189–1204. https://doi.org/10.1037/a0029356

Darling-Hammond, L., Holtzman, D. J., Gatlin, S., & Vasquez Heilig, J. (2005). Does teacher preparation matter? Evidence about teacher certification, teach for America, and teacher effectiveness. Education Policy Analysis Archives, 13(42), 1-51 http://www.redalyc.org/articulo.oa?id=275020513042

Delali, O., Zungbey, D., Sokro, E., Akomeah, M., Ntow, O., & Osei-Bonsu, N. (2020). Emotional labour and turnover intention among teachers: The moderating role of team support. In (Ed.), Advances in intelligent systems and computing (pp. 131–142). Springer International Publishing. https://doi.org/10.1007/978-3-030-50791-6_17

Eatough, E. M., Meier, L. L., Igic, I., Elfering, A., Spector, P. E., & Semmer, N. K. (2015). You want me to do what? Two daily diary studies of illegitimate tasks and employee well-being. Journal of Organizational Behavior, 37(1), 108–127. https://doi.org/10.1002/job.2032

Edinger, S. K., & Edinger, M. J. (2018). Improving teacher job satisfaction: The roles of

    social capital, teacher efficacy, and support. The Journal of Psychology, 152(8),

    573–593. https://doi.org/10.1080/00223980.2018.1489364

Education Code Chapter 29. Educational Programs. (2021, September 1). Sec. 29.001.

    https://statutes.capitol.texas.gov/Docs/ED/htm/ED.29.htm

    Grantham-Caston, M., & DiCarlo, C. (2021). Leadership styles in childcare directors. Early

    Childhood Education Journal, 51, 105-114. https://doi.org/10.1007/s10643-021-01282-2

Hart, K., & Schumacher, R. (2005, July). Making the case: Improving head start teacher

    qualifications requires increased investment. CLASP.

    https://www.clasp.org/publications/ report/brief/making-case-improving-head-start-teacher-

    qualifications-requires-increased

Haslip, M. J., & Gullo, D. F. (2017). The changing landscape of early childhood education:

    Implications for policy and practice. Early Childhood Education Journal, 46(3),

    249–264. https://doi.org/10.1007/s10643-017-0865-7

Hudson, D. (2015, May 18). This day in history: The creation of head start. The White

    House. https://obamawhitehouse.archives.gov/blog/2015/05/18/day-his

    tory-creation-head-start

Jacoby, J., & Lesaux, N. K. (2017). Policy-based instructional reform in early education:

    How us head start teachers perceive instructional mandates. International Journal of

    Child Care and Education Policy, 11(1). https://doi.org/10.1186/s40723-017-0034-x

Jeon, L., & Wells, M. B. (2018). An organizational-level analysis of early childhood

    teachers' job attitudes: Workplace satisfaction affects early head start and head start

    teacher turnover. Child & Youth Care Forum, 47(4), 563–581.

    https://doi.org/10.1007/s10566-018-9444-3

Lieberman, A. (2017, May 17). A tale of two pre-k leaders. New America.

   https://www.newamerica.org/education-policy/policy-papers/tale-two-pre-k-leaders/

Maslow, A. H. (1943). A theory of human motivation. Psychological Review, 50(4), 370–

   396. https://doi.org/10.1037/h0054346

Maxwell, J. (2022, August). Special teaching with John Maxwell [Conference session].

   International Maxwell Conference, Orlando, FL, United States.

McMullen, M. B., Lee, M. C., McCormick, K. I., & Choi, J. (2020). Early childhood

   professional well-being as a predictor of the risk of turnover in childcare: A matter of

   quality. Journal of Research in Childhood Education, 34(3), 331–345.

   https://doi.org/10.1080/02568543.2019.1705446

Myers, A. (2021, October 21). Heading off head start educator burnout. The Hub.

   https://hub.jhu.edu/2021/10/21/head-start-educator-burnout/

Northouse, P. G. (2019). Leadership: Theory and practice (8th ed.). SAGE Publications, Inc.

   Office of Head Start. (2021, April 4). U.S. Department of Health & Human Services.

   https://www.acf.hhs.gov/ohs/about/history-head-start

Pomaki, G., DeLongis, A., Frey, D., Short, K., & Woehrle, T. (2010). When the going gets

   tough: Direct, buffering and indirect effects of social support on turnover intention.

   Teaching and Teacher Education, 26(6), 1340–1346.

   https://doi.org/10.1016/j.tate.2010.03.007

Skaalvik, E. M., & Skaalvik, S. (2011). Teacher job satisfaction and motivation to leave the

   teaching profession: Relations with school context, feeling of belonging, and

   emotional exhaustion. Teaching and Teacher Education, 27(6), 1029–1038.

   https://doi.org/10.1016/j.tate.2011.04.001

Smith, J., Blevins, B., Werse, N. R., & Talbert, S. (2020). Researcher positionality in the
dissertation in practice. In Practice-based and practice-led research for dissertation
development (p. 15). IGI Global. https://doi.org/10.4018/978-1-7998-6664-0.ch003

U.S. Department of Health and Human Services. (2007, December). Head Start policy and
regulations. Head Start/ECLKC https://eclkc.ohs.acf.hhs.gov/policy/
head-start-act/sec-648a-staff-qualifications-development

U.S. Department of Health and Human Services. (2007, December). Head start program
performance standards. Head Start/ECLKC https://eclkc.ohs.acf.hhs.gov/poli
cy/45-cfr-chap-xiii/1302-21-center-based-option

U.S. Department of Health and Human Services. (2022). Welcome to HSES. Office of Head
Start/Head Start enterprise system. https://hses.ohs.acf.hhs.gov

Wells, M. B. (2015). Predicting preschool teacher retention and turnover in newly hired head
start teachers across the first half of the school year. Early Childhood Research
Quarterly, 30, 152–159. https://doi.org/10.1016/j.ecresq.2014.10.003

Whitebook, M., Phillips, D., & Howes, C. (2014). Worthy work, still unlivable wages: The
early childhood workforce 25 years after the national childcare staffing study. UC
Berkeley: Center for the Study of Childcare Employment.
https://escholarship.org/uc/item/16

www.ingramcontent.com/pod-product-compliance
Lightning Source LLC
Chambersburg PA
CBHW080957120626
46546CB00010B/2935